T0266054

MYSTICAL
CRYSTALS

Also by Cerridwen Greenleaf

*Moon Spell Magic for Love: Charms, Invocations,
Passion Potions, and Rituals for Romance*

*Moon Spell Magic: Invocations, Incantations
& Lunar Lore for a Happy Life*

*Dark Moon Magic: Supernatural Spells, Charms,
and Rituals for Health, Wealth, and Happiness*

*The Magic of Crystals & Gems: Unlocking the
Supernatural Power of Stones*

*The Magic Oracle Book: Ask Any Question and
Discover Your Fate*

*The Practical Witch's Spell Book: For Love,
Happiness, and Success*

*5-Minute Magic for Modern Wiccans: Rapid Rituals,
Efficient Enchantments, and Swift Spells*

MYSTICAL CRYSTALS

Magical Stones and Gems for Health, Wealth and Happiness

CERRIDWEN GREENLEAF

TURNER
PUBLISHING COMPANY

Turner Publishing Company
Nashville, Tennessee
www.turnerpublishing.com

Cover, Layout & Design: Morgane Leoni

Library of Congress Cataloging-in-Publication number: 2019948620
ISBN: (print) 978-1-64250-095-0, (e) 978-1-64250-189-6
BISAC OCC004000, BODY, MIND & SPIRIT / Crystals

Printed in the United States of America

Contents

Introduction

CRYSTAL
CHEMISTRY—**HOW**
THEY WORK AND
WHY THEY WORK

Welcome to the wonderful world of gems and crystals! Together we are going to explore this glittery realm, and you will discover which stones are exactly right for you. Certain stones will bring love into your life, other crystals are calming, and particular gems will heal your body and provide you with a deep sense of well-being. Still others will help you get to the depth of your personal creativity and stimulate your mind.

This book is organized to help you apply crystal self-care to your daily life. You will also learn how to make your own jewelry and utilize wellness tools, including lucky amulets and salt crystal lamps, and all manner of marvelous minerals to enhance every aspect of your life.

Crystals can truly enhance your life, and I have long enjoyed the benefits. Gems have gotten me through heartache and helped me find new and true love. They have aided me in finding work and achieving abundance and prosperity in my life. I keep crystals on my desk to help me focus, on my nightstand to abet sleep, and around the house for health and happiness. In *Mystical Crystals*, you can discover which crystals are right for *you*.

Garnet

Chapter 1

BIRTHSTONE SECRETS—DISCOVERING YOUR SOUL STONES

Birthstones are very special stones that have traditionally been correlated with each month of the year. Hallmark didn't invent the concept of birthstones; it came from the Bible! In Exodus chapters twenty-eight and thirty-nine, there is much discussion about a burnished and stone-set breastplate of the High Priest of the Hebrews. Here is the biblical description of the breastplate:

And he made the breastplate, artistically woven like the workmanship of the ephod, of gold, blue, purple, and scarlet thread, and of fine woven linen. They made the breastplate square by doubling it; a span was its length and a span its width when doubled. And they set in it four rows of stones: the first row with a sardius, a topaz, and an emerald; the second row, a turquoise, a sapphire, and a diamond; the third row, a jacinth, an agate, and an amethyst; the fourth row, a beryl, an onyx, and a jasper. They were enclosed in settings of gold in their mountings. There were twelve stones according to the names of the sons of Israel: according to their names, engraved like a signet, each one with its own name according to the twelve tribes.

—NKJV, Exod. 39:8–14

Amethyst

These twelve stones from the famous breastplate became linked with the twelve signs of the zodiac, resulting in our cherished modern tradition of birthstones. The long history of birthstones has many more chapters, but an important point to know is that your birthstone is yours by divine right and birthright. I know I was thrilled when I found out amethyst was mine, even though it was ranked as semiprecious. All I knew was that it was purple, my favorite color.

Your birthstone is a major power source for you. You should have at least one piece of jewelry made from your birthstone and must treat it like the special stone it is. You should also keep this sacred personal stone around in other forms as well. I have a candleholder made of a large amethyst geode on my mantelpiece surrounded by candles. Just lighting the candle immediately calms and centers me. I realize you can't do that with diamonds, although Herkimer diamonds can be substituted nicely. If you are a January Capricorn, for instance, and your birthstone is garnet, you can have an entire set, or parure, of garnet jewelry—ring, earrings, bracelet, necklace—for the fullest expression of birthstone power. Surround yourself with your birthstone energy and you will feel at peace, filled with well-being from your gem-fired glow.

Ruby

Here is the classic list of birthstones by month.

- **January:** garnet, a stone symbolizing a light and loyal heart and lasting affection

- **February:** amethyst, a sexy and sensitive stone; Cleopatra's royal ring

- **March:** aquamarine, long known as a soothsayer's stone; and bloodstone, long known as the martyr's stone

- **April:** diamond, the traditional engagement ring, which represents the power of love

- **May:** emerald, a lovely green stone of protection

- **June:** pearl, moonstone, and alexandrite—all moon and sea stones powered by water

- **July:** ruby, the most highly prized gem of all and a symbol of the essence of life

- **August:** peridot, the ancient symbol of the sun; and sardonyx, an intelligence-enhancing stone

- **September:** sapphire, a true-blue gem that represents the purity of the soul

- **October:** opal, said to contain the beauty of all other gems; and tourmaline, a stone of inspiration

- **November:** topaz, a stone of royalty, named for the Sanskrit word for fire
- **December:** turquoise, which brings luck; and zircon, the traveler's stone

While the classic birthstones are, well, classic, each zodiac sign has "early" and "late" divisions, and each of those has heart-, soul-, and power-correlated stones. Check for your and your loved ones' birthdays below to see which gems will rev up different areas of your lives!

Opal

Aries,

First Half: March 20–April 3

Sunstone

The sunstone is the power crystal for these Aries folks. Appropriately red with an iridescent glow, sunstone is a gold-flecked good-luck charm for the Mars-ruled. Jasper and heliotrope are the other power stones for this part of the year. These red rocks will amp up your lust for life.

The heart stones for these zodiac pioneers are dolomite, rose quartz, and cinnabar. So, Aries, put a rose quartz by your bedside for self-esteem, self-love, and spiritual comfort.

Aries,

Last Half: April 4–April 18

Bowenite

Alexandrite is the designated soul stone here. It is very precious indeed—the scarcest of the chrysoberyls. Usually a dark green, alexandrite shows red under certain types of light. This royal stone is fitting for the first sign of the zodiac. Another soul stone for later-born Aries is rhodonite, a pinkish red crystal that's a favorite of Carl Faberge's.

The power stone for this half of Aries is bowenite, a stone of great strength in a mossy green. While many of the crystals assigned to late Aries are red or pink, this one is green, signifying the other side of the planet Mars. Bowenite is especially precious and sacred to the Maori of New Zealand, where some of the finest specimens come from, and was highly prized by the ancient Indians and Persians.

Taurus,

First Half: April 19–May 2

Pyrite

The power stone for this group is another gorgeous green stone: malachite, which also corresponds to the planet Venus. An earthy rock, it is befitting for this earth sign of the zodiac and has many magical tales to its name. A malachite heart pendant or paperweight is perfect for early Tauruses.

Pyrite, or fool's gold, is the heart stone for people in this family, who tend to be bankers and money managers. Stunning and shiny, pyrite has a hardness of six, the number sacred to Venus. Pyrite brings great luck to early Tauruses, along with abundance and an atmosphere conducive to joy. Delight everyone at work by keeping a chunk of fool's gold on your desk.

Taurus,

Second Half: May 3–May 19

Andalusite

Andalusite is the precious soul stone here, a magically metamorphic crystal. Tauruses are deeply rooted to the earth, and andalusite represents that elemental energy through its range of colors, from earthy black to clear and watery. In fact, andalusite comes in nearly all the colors of the rainbow (yellow, green, red, purple, brown, and gray), manifesting another Venusian quality—glamour.

Jadeite, the power stone for later Tauruses, also comes in many colors. Jadeite is a symbol for abundance and permanence. It rings with a lovely tone when struck, representing the natural musical talent possessed by members of this sign. A jadeite bracelet, ring, or bowl is essential for the May-born.

Gemini,

First Half: May 20–June 4

Staurolite

Moss agate, quartz with a plantlike pattern caused by metallic crystalline grains, is the power stone for first-half Geminis and represents the dualism of this sign of the twins. The ancients thought the dark-green markings inside the stone were fossilized moss. They used moss agate for water divining, so it was especially sacred to farmers. It is associated with the metal-rich planet Mercury and makes a great grounding stone for members of this air sign, who need to keep their feet on the ground.

The heart stone for early Geminis is staurolite, derived from the Greek word *staurus*, which translates to "cross." Staurolite forms a natural crucifix because of the way the iron molecules in the stone line up. Bright red is one of the colors associated with Geminis, and staurolite most commonly appears in this vibrant color, causing it to be mistaken for garnet. This stone can help Geminis align with their true purpose, so they will benefit from keeping it at their bedsides or on their desks.

Gemini,

Second Half: June 5–June 20

Geode

Cat's-eye, the lovely golden-yellow gem, is the special soul stone for late-born Geminis. The ancient Greeks, who called this crystal *cymophane*, meaning "waving light," believed this stone guarded against danger to the soul and the body. The iridescent surface of the stone causes it to appear in different colors; the shade depends on the angle from which the cat's-eye is being seen. This mutable stone reflects back to Geminis their changeable nature and helps them to acknowledge their quicksilver personalities and to grow from that deep recognition. Geminis, wear a cat's-eye ring and see your soul reflected back at you.

Geodes, which usually come in two split halves, are the ideal heart stones for later-born Geminis, but they must have both halves to help integrate the two parts of their nature into a complete, whole person. Geodes are formed from old volcanic bubbles and are usually solid agate on the outside with a center of gorgeous amethyst, opal, or rock crystal. If you are a Gemini, I recommend keeping one of the geode halves at home on your altar, or in a special spot where you can see it every day, and the other half at your place of work, to reflect on and connect the two parts of your nature.

Cancer,

First Half: June 21–July 4

Moonstone

Cancers are ruled by the Moon, so it is appropriate that the moonstone is the precious soul stone for the individuals born in the first half of this sign. The most priceless of moonstones is adularia, named after the place it was first discovered—Adula, Switzerland. Adularia was special to early Europeans who believed it could improve the memory, help stop seizures, overcome a broken heart, and foretell the future. Wearing moonstone jewelry will put Cancers in tune with their lunar-influenced changeable natures, giving them strength and the wisdom of intuition.

Pearl is the power stone of great price for early Cancers. Pearls have a long and rich history; they were first written about in China four thousand years ago. Cancers are the great historians of the zodiac, and they have incredible memories. They are connected to pearls because of a common link with the ocean and the tides, which are regulated by Cancer's ruler, the moon. If you are a Cancer, honor your native element, water, by wearing pearls on occasion (but not constantly) and by decorating your home and work space with shells. This will help you stay secure, refreshed, and relaxed and help you avoid your great nemesis—worry.

Cancer,

Second Half: July 5–July 21

Desert Rose

Opal is the soul stone for later-born Cancers. Opals can't be duplicated artificially due to their varying hues, play of color, and the complicated nature of their patterning. The most precious of all opals feature a star, called an asterism. Opals are mysterious, just like Cancers, having much depth beneath their protective shells. The ancients exulted about opals; Pliny the Elder wrote, "For in them you shall see the living fire of ruby, the glorious purple of the amethyst, the sea-green of the emerald, all glittering together in an incredible mixture of light." Cancers, you will come into your soul's true purpose by wearing opal jewelry.

Desert rose, formed of cemented sand particles, is the heart stone for this group of Cancers. The Saharan Bedouin believed it was formed from the tears of women mourning for those who had died in battle. Originated in lake bottoms that have become deserts, desert rose is gypsum that comes in beautiful earth tones of red, yellow, gray, brown, and pink. For later Cancers, this heart stone helps contain and release emotions in a healthy, expressive way. Decorate your bedroom, your inner sanctum, with desert rose for a soothing and calming effect.

Leo,

First Half: July 22–August 5

Zircon

First-half Leos can count zircon as their power stone. Beloved by early cultures, the brilliant zircon was believed to safeguard against poison and was thought to be a holy healer in India. In the early Roman Catholic church, it was the sign of humility. For Leos, whose downfall can be pride, zircon can guard against this and keep the astrological Lions on an even keel.

Early-born Leos have a special heart stone in lesser-known vandanite, which can be a beautiful red orange or a glorious yellow gold. Vanadinite is rich in lead and vanadium, the mineral used to strengthen steel. Vanadinite is formed at intense temperatures, which can be related to our sun, a furnace in the heavens. For Leos, this unusual heart stone can help them deal with the pressure of a lot of attention, which Leos naturally attract with their vibrant and magnetic personalities. You should keep your heart stone at home and at work for optimum stability and inspiration.

Leo,

Second Half: August 6–August 21

Heliodor

Heliodor, named for Helios, the Greek god of the sun, is the ultimate power stone for second-half Leos. Heliodor, a member of the beryl family, is the sunny yellow sister of the popular green emerald and blue aquamarine. It is formed under extremely high temperatures and pressures. Heliodor can help you Leos call upon your greatest qualities and talents and provide the impetus to go out and make your dreams come true!

The heart stone for later-born Leos is the most unexpected—sulfur, called brimstone in biblical times. Sulfur is a very dynamic rock; the crystals enlarge even from the heat of a hand holding it. If you rub sulfur, it will give off a negative charge. A cluster of sulfur is a luminous mass of gold crystals and is quite beautiful, despite the images its name may conjure. Obviously, sulfur is associated with fire and has been used for centuries in explosive materials such as gunpowder, fireworks, and matches. Leo is a fire sign, and Leos can hold emotions in until they ignite and explode. Keeping sulfur at home can help Leos stay balanced and release their energy in healthy and positive ways.

Virgo,

First Half: August 22–September 5

Magnetite

The power talisman for first-half Virgos is labradorite, a lovely iridescent stone that originated in Labrador. Like Geminis, Virgos are ruled by Mercury, and the quicksilver, peacock-hued labradorite is good for providing the mental swiftness Virgos need to accomplish all of their goals in life. This type of feldspar can reflect every color of the spectrum and help Virgos from becoming too task oriented—too focused on one thing. No one can work harder than Virgos, so labradorite can prevent exhaustion from overwork and can also ensure that early Virgos activate a variety of talents.

Magnetite, also known as lodestone, is the optimal heart stone for first-half Virgos. Another glittery, surface-changing rock, magnetite contains a lot of iron and, thanks to its common occurrence and adaptability, is popular in jewelry. Virgos are associated with health, medicine, and nursing, and magnetite has become a good healing stone because of its magnetic qualities. If you are a Virgo, wear this stone and give it to people you love for good health and prosperity.

Virgo,

Second Half: September 6–September 21

Iolite

Virgos in this group celebrate iolite as their precious soul gem, which is associated with their ruling planet Mercury due to its crystalline composition of two dark and two light metallic elements. Iolite is named after the Greek word *ios*, meaning "violet." Formed under enormous pressure in extremely high temperatures, iolite has high vibration. The stone can help Virgos stay out of career ruts and achieve their true spiritual natures.

The heart stone for second-half Virgos is obsidian, a glinting black and extremely hard natural glass formed by volcanic activity. Virgos are always helping other people and sometimes become vulnerable because of this. Using obsidian pieces as home decorations can help them keep all of their energy from going to others and causing imbalance. Some obsidian samples have stripes; in ancient Mexico, where obsidian was plentiful, the striped variety was believed to prevent negative, or dark, magic. Virgos can be extremely self-critical, and having obsidian nearby can absorb their negativity and help turn it positive. This is an essential stone for the September-born!

Libra,

First Half: September 22–October 6

Kyanite

Dioptase is the power stone for first-half Libras. A deeper green than any emerald, it has an extensive copper content. Venus is associated with the color green, and the intensity of this gorgeous green stone makes it a love crystal for Venus-ruled Libras, enriching both their personal relationships and their higher love for humankind. Dioptase can also awaken the spiritual side of Libras, making the usually attractive members of this sign even more beautiful inside and out. Dioptase is difficult to cut for jewelry because of its brittleness. Use uncut crystal clusters as lovely spirit enhancers all around the home.

Kyanite is the sky-colored heart stone for early Libras and is known as a stone of symmetry, perfect for providing balance. The Greeks favored this aluminum-based rock and called it disthene, meaning "dual strength," because it is soft (and easily cut) lengthwise but much harder across. Kyanite most commonly occurs in long, bluish-green crystal blades but also in cluttered rosettes with a pearly, opalescent surface. If you're a Libra, an air sign, keep kyanite around to stay steady and strong and help avoid spreading yourself too thin and succumbing to petty, energy-draining distractions.

Libra,

Second Half: October 7–October 22

Jadeite

The power talisman for this group of Libras is jadeite, sometimes called imperial green jade. The Chinese have prized this stone highly throughout their culture's lengthy history and believe it contains all that you need for a happy, long life—courage, modesty, charity, wisdom, and, most important for the Libra scales to be in balance, justice. Jade bookends on your desk are perfect balancers.

Limonite, an icicle-like mineral appearing in long, shiny pieces, is the heart stone for second-half Libras. This represents the striving for higher mind, higher beauty, and higher love necessary for the completion of Libra karma.

Scorpio,

First Half: October 23–November 6

Stibnite

First-half Scorpios have a most unusual power stone in Blue John. It is found in only one place in the world: the underground caverns beneath a hill in the county of Derbyshire, England. Its appearance of dark-blue and reddish-purple bands on a white background relates to Pluto, the second ruling planet of Scorpio, which is the sign of the underworld and secrets. Though Blue John can be difficult to come by, other fluorites are more readily available and will substitute nicely for the rare stone. Fluorite is thought to be healing to the bones and to wounds that lie underneath the surface. Secretive Scorpios carry many hurts beneath strong exteriors, and fluorites can gently resolve these over time.

For early Scorpios, the heart stone is stibnite, a blue-gray mineral that comes in clusters of needle-like rods. Stibnite is closely associated with Pluto and has a shiny and opalescent surface. It is soft, and, because of its crumbliness, stibnite makes it easier for Scorpios to get along with other people and get along better in the world. If you're a Scorpio, you know you have a strong will; this stone can help you get your ideas across without forcing them. A chunk of stibnite on your desk at work will help your career and reputation.

Scorpio,

Second Half: November 7–November 21

Quartz crystal

Everybody thinks of amethyst as the February crystal for Aquarians and Pisceans, but it is also the power stone for second-half Scorpios. The purple color relates to the purple planet, Pluto. Amethysts can open the love vibration for individuals ruled by this most misunderstood and enormously powerful water sign. Wearing amethyst jewelry and keeping chunks of amethyst crystal in the home and workplace can reveal the sweet, funny, smart, approachable, and lovable side of Scorpios, offering them a much greater chance for happiness.

Scorpios have their heart stone in the very available quartz crystal. Quartz is a tremendous healer and so are Scorpios, though they rarely receive credit for this latent talent. When a Scorpio puts her mind to something, nothing can stand in the way! By acknowledging and utilizing the healing power of quartz crystals, Scorpios can use their personal power for the good of others and greatly benefit. Surround yourself with this inexpensive heat crystal and feel the love.

Sagittarius,

First Half: November 22–December 5

Tourmaline

Tourmaline—specifically the multihued specimen known as melonstone, which is pinkish red with a blue-green stripe—is the precious soul stone for the Jupiter-ruled Sagittarians. Individuals under this fire sign are lively and very action-oriented, and tourmaline, which readily gives off an electrical charge when warmed, can match and propel their energy. Tourmaline is the stone for adventurers and explorers. Get some today and hit the road, dear Sag.

Chrysocolla is the heart stone for first-half Sagittarians. Either blue or green, this copper-rich crystal is one of great life-giving vibrancy. Sagittarians always have many irons in many fires and often burn up their energy in typical fire-sign style. Chrysocolla can help prevent this and help Sagittarians direct their energy toward more purposeful and heartfelt pursuits.

Sagittarius,

Second Half: December 6–December 20

Bornite

Turquoise is this group's power stone. The rock has a rich and colorful history and was valued in the extreme by Persians, Egyptians, Mexicans, Bedouins, Chinese, Tibetans, Native Americans, and Turks. Turquoise is associated with horses and riders; Sagittarius is the centaur of the zodiac—half man and half horse. Once revered as the eye of Ra, the Egyptian sun-god, turquoise lends sight and aids in travel. Wearing this stone will help people born in this part of the year find their purpose and harness the passion and vision to see it through.

The heart stone for second-half Sagittarians is bornite, a burnished red rock of copper and iron. Bornite used to be called peacock ore because of its impressive iridescent coloration. It is a very powerful energy crystal. Although it is not widely known, Sagittarians can be indecisive, and this stone abets them in overcoming that. This is also a stone of justice, and Jupiter-ruled Sagittarians are lovers of justice.

Capricorn,

First Half: December 21–January 6

Citrine

For power stones, first-half Goats have both lazulite and jet, gems that have a dark and shadowy appearance representative of Saturn, Capricorn's ruling planet. Jet is one of the oldest stones known to man, fitting with the longevity of the slow and steady Capricorns, who are reputed to grow more youthful as they get older. Wear jet to live long and prosper!

Citrine and smoky quartz are the heart stones for this sector of the zodiac and will ground this hardworking earth sign. Keep citrine at your place of work and wear citrine rings and necklaces frequently to remain in touch with your feelings.

Capricorn,

Second Half: January 7–January 19

Lapis Lazuli

Tanzanite is the sacred soul stone for these Capricorns. A gorgeous purple stone found in 1967 Tanzania, it corresponds to the ruling planet of Saturn. Appropriately regal and rare, it is as serious as the sign it signifies. For important meetings and moments in your life, a tanzanite jewel will make you a shining star!

Lucky Goats in the latter half of Capricorn get to have lapis lazuli as their talismanic power crystal. This crystal was absolutely revered by the Egyptians and other Mesopotamian cultures. A bright blue, this stone connotes wisdom, accomplishment, and value. I highly suggest lots of lapis boxes, jewelry, and figurines.

Aquarius,

First Half: January 20–February 3

Moldavite

Olivine is the soul gem of choice for first half Aquarians, and it is a stone with a royal heritage. The Egyptians believed this peridot to be the stone of the gods. The long, convoluted, and quite bizarre history of this stone entirely suits Aquarians, who are ruled by Uranus, the planet of chaos and unexpected change. Wear a dark-green olivine on momentous occasions to mark them as special in your life.

The heart stone for this group is moldavite. With its otherworldly meteorite origin, it is perfect for the Uranian bolt-from-the-blue these scientist-philosophers represent. Moldavite is a mysterious and powerful crystal with many mist-shrouded legends and theories. No doubt, an Aquarius will get to the bottom of them all, one day. Moldavite will add to your Aquarian brilliance and boost your personal creativity to new heights.

Aquarius,

Second Half: February 4–February 18

Diopside

Diopside is the beautiful blue soul stone for later-born Aquarians. This stone has ties to both Uranus, the official ruling planet of Aquarius, and Saturn, the sign's ruler before Uranus was discovered. In 1964, star diopside, an included type, was found; it is a magical and stunningly gorgeous stone that has a quality of electric enlightenment, just like these February-born inventors, artists, and visionary businesspeople.

The heart stone for second-half Aquarians is charoite, a purple mineral that corresponds with Venus, Saturn, and Uranus. This is a fairly recent rock, perfect for the modern-minded February-born, who are generally fifty years ahead of everyone else. Charoite was discovered circa 1947 near the Chara River in Russia and was immediately greeted as a very special stone for modern history.

Pisces,

First Half: February 19–March 4

Smithsonite

For their power talisman, early Pisceans have a mutable rock: smithsonite, a soft, calcium-based stone that comes in a variety of lovely pastel colors. It is a stone for creativity, the bailiwick of this sign. Keep smithsonite at your easel, drawing table, or writing desk.

Opal fossils, the heart stones for these sensitive people, are ancient fragments that crystallized and achieved iridescence through an accumulation of water and minerals over time. Pisces is, of course, a water sign and is also associated with history and deep, old wisdom.

Pisces,

Second Half: March 5–March 19

Fluorite

The power stone for late Pisces is the chrysoprase, a gem that has been revered throughout the ages. Chrysoprase was assigned sovereignty and utilized by high priests of nearly every era. This crystal is perfect for the sign that can attain the highest level of spiritual evolution. With chrysoprase, you can help others and yourself through soul attunement.

Late Pisceans can count as their heart stone the all-purpose fluorite, which comes in a rainbow of colors corresponding to the rainbow gills of fish. This stone is found all over our planet and is so universally helpful that it presents a solid foundation for gentle Pisceans. Fluorite at home and work will add comfort and grace to your space.

RINGS OF REJUVENATION

Gemstones and crystals have transformative powers and magic that has been worked with since olden days. Bring birthstone blessings into your life by using these Rings of Rejuvenation.

Sapphire has violet energy. Worn on the first Saturday of the month on the middle finger of the right hand two hours before sunset, the stone is said to be a curative for kidney ailments, epilepsy, tumors, and sciatica.

Diamond, which contains rays of indigo light, is good for maintaining the health of the eyes and nose, managing asthma and laziness, and maintaining sobriety, especially if worn on the right pinkie on Friday during the waxing moon.

Emerald has green light rays and can help with the heart, ulcers, cancer, asthma, and influenza. Wear emerald on the right pinkie on Wednesday two hours after dawn.

Pearls radiate orange rays and operate as a curative if worn on Monday morning by the individual afflicted with insanity, diabetes, colic, or fever.

Topaz has blue rays and helps with laryngitis, paralysis, hysteria, scarlet fever, and assorted glandular disorders if worn on the right ring finger on Thursday mornings.

Chapter 2

TRANQUILITY TOUCHSTONES—
STRESS-REDUCING
ROCKS

Crystals found in nature are imbued with special qualities from the minerals and rocks surrounding them. Geologists are fond of explaining the varying colors of crystals as chemical impurities, and, while that may well be so, I prefer to liken the development of crystalline color to the making of a fine wine, wherein the soil, neighboring trees, plants, sun, and rain affect the grapes and the resulting nectar. Gems have notes, like perfume or wine or even music. Truly gifted gemologists can distinguish these delicate differences, especially the vibratory sounds.

Using gems and crystals in rituals, shrines, and affirmations has been part of the human experience for millennia. By incorporating this practice into your life, you will create a flow of positive energy that will enable you to decrease stress and increase positivity and serenity.

Pink Agate

Energy Management—You and Your Crystals

The first thing you need to do with a crystal is *charge* it, which means syncing it up with your personal frequency and vibrations. You're placing your desires and wishes into the vessel of the crystal. The crystal's inherent energies will come into play with your personal power, and your intentions can be manifested, or made real, through the crystal.

The very first step in this process, however, is the dedication of the crystal toward the greater good of all beings. An essential part of this process is the cleansing of the crystal in order to purify its energy. Although this is a straight-forward task, it is of supreme importance for your use of the crystal down the road. If a gem or stone is not as effective as you had hoped, the problem could stem from the initial dedication. Think of this primary step as the honing and direction of the intention. Here is how: simply hold the crystal in the palm of your right hand, and in your mind picture a glow of light surrounding the stone.

When the rock is completely enveloped by light in your mind's eye, state out loud, "This crystal is only for exacting good of the highest order. In this stone of the earth, there is only love and light." I like to leave the crystal out in the light of the natural rays of the sun and the moon for a twenty-four-hour period for the maximum dedication of light and love from the universe and the heavens above as part of the purification process. But, if time is of the essence, you can move right on to step number two, charging the crystal itself.

All stones possess natural energies of their very own. You want to merge your energies with those of your crystals so that the crystals will be in sync with your vibratory channel. Remain mindful of the great power your stones have and you will be in a good position to work with it. Consider carefully what kind of energy you want to place into your crystal. Take a stone that has been cleansed by sitting in a bowl of sea salt overnight and in the light of the sun for a day. Sit in a comfortable position and hold the crystal in your right hand. Focus on the energy you desire your crystal to hold and project it into the stone. Bear in mind, the use of crystal magic should not be used solely for your purposes, but also for the greater good. Please make sure you're projecting positive energy and not anger or hatred. You should ask aloud for your crystal to work together with you for the highest good. You are doing creative visualization here, so keep concentrating until you can see and feel the energy flowing into the stone. You will feel when the charging, or programming, is complete; your intuition will tell you.

While it is not the best-case scenario, you can charge a stone for someone else. For example, if you have a friend who is very ill and halfway around the world, you could charge the crystal with positive, healing energy and send it to your friend to help them. Ask the crystal to work for the highest good of this person and then release that crystal to them.

MYSTICAL CRYSTAL DIY: PARKING PENDANT

Hang a red jasper crystal attached to a string on your rearview mirror in your car and your parking problems will soon be over. When you need a spot, touch the jasper and say, "Squat, Squat, find me a spot!" Remember to always give thanks to the parking gods and goddesses to remain in their favor.

Stress-Reducing Stones

Alexandrite will bring lots of zest. Feeling depressed, worried, and blue? Citrine or jet can banish dark days. Stressed out? Rhyolite races to the rescue as well.

Alexandrite

Certain green stones, such as chrysocolla and malachite, calm the mind, and green-flecked bloodstone is a stress buffer.

Green-flecked bloodstone

If you want to be uplifted, try jade. To become wiser, pick sapphire. To stay safe while traveling, pick dendritic agate.

Raw sapphire

To remain calm and overcome stress, choose blue lace agate. For more mental clarity, choose malachite. For a self-esteem boost, try rhodonite.

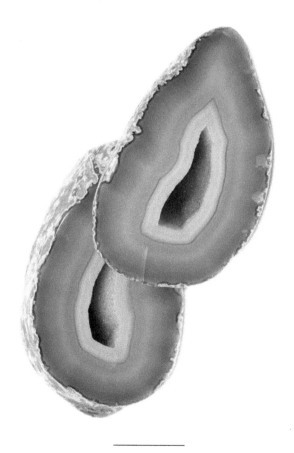

Blue lace agate

Herkimer diamonds are powerful and bring great vitality and exuberance into your life. They can redirect stress away from you with their absorptive abilities. Placing these rocks in your bedroom will cause the stress to melt away and help you relax and feel safe.

Herkimer diamonds

Dioptase is a gorgeous gemstone that nearly matches the color of green emeralds but lacks a similar hardness, which lowers its marketplace value. It can be found in Peru, Chile, Russia, Iran, and some sites in Africa. The true value of dioptase lies in its ability to help anyone experiencing mental stress. It lends balance to male and female energies and acts as a stabilizer. As an energy stone, dioptase can activate and awaken every chakra, invigorating the mind, body, and spirit. If you want to be really different, wear dioptase, and you will fascinate admirers with this beautiful stone and find peace of mind in the process.

Dioptase

WRITTEN IN STONE

Gems and crystals can give us messages and warnings or powers of persuasion and perception. Here are a few examples:

- A fossil or a gem containing a fossil, such as amber, will lengthen your life span.

- Jasper carved into the shape of an arrow will be a magnet for good luck.

- If your malachite jewelry chips or breaks, beware! It is warning you of danger.

- Malachite gives great success to salespeople. Keep a malachite crystal in the cash register and wear it during trade shows, presentations, and meetings.

- Moonstone is the dieter's power stone and helps maintain youthful appearances and attitudes.

- Serpentine worn around a new mother's neck helps her flow of milk.

Stone of Self-Belief: Hematite Vanquishes Anxiety

Hematite shores up self-image and self-belief. It also transforms negative energy into positive. Hematite is considered to be yang, a more male energy. My favorite aspect of this shiny wonder is that it assists with both legal problems and astral projection. Hematite is a creativity crystal and a marvelous mental enhancer, increasing the ability to focus, concentrate, think with logic, and remember more clearly and completely. Hematite draws anxiety out of the body and creates calm. In addition to all of these aspects that project outward, hematite contributes to inner work: self-knowledge, deeper consciousness, and wisdom. Like the iron in the earth from which it is formed, hematite grounds. If you feel spacey or disconnected, you should wear hematite.

Hematite

Self-Esteem Stones: Raise Your Spirits with Rose

If you want to jump-start your life and bring about positive change, tap into the power of rose and red stones. Stones of this side of the color spectrum contain life's energy and can help you become more motivated, energetic, and vibrant, as well as give you an appealing aura. Wear this list of rosy and red stones, or place them on your desk and throughout your home for an instant boost: alexandrite, carnelian, garnet, red coral, red jasper, rhyolite, rose jasper, and ruby.

Red jasper

Lepidolite—Let Go of Your Worries Stone

Lepidolite should be called the letting-go stone. It's like a fresh breeze coming into a room filled with stale air. In elixir form, it's a wonderful way to deal with addictive behavior or to rid yourself of old patterns that no longer serve you or are potentially unhealthy. This uncommon mica, an ore of lithium, has only recently come onto the gem and mineral market. It is shiny and plate-like in appearance, usually occurring in a pretty, pearly pink or purple color. On occasion, it appears white, and, very rarely, it shows up in gray or yellow. This mineral occurs in Brazil, Russia, California, and a few spots throughout Africa. My favorite specimens are the single, large sheets of the lovely mica, which are called books and are an unforgettable violet.

Lepidolite is a great stone for getting a handle on anger issues. It soothes unresolved resentments, hatred, and frustrations. It is another mental stone and amplifies thoughts. Lepidolite is almost like a fairy stone in that it attracts positive energy, brightens spirits, and increases intuition. This is one powerful chakra healer, particularly for the heart and root chakras. One of the most important uses for this stone, albeit with great care, is for healing issues resulting from incest. Lepidolite is so powerful that it can be a tool for those dealing with manic depression.

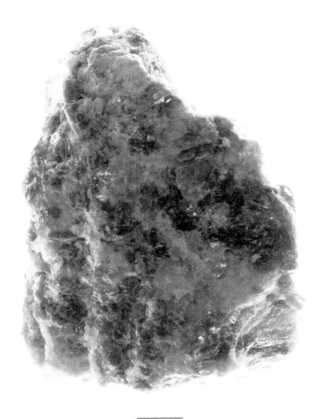

Lepidolite

JEWELS OF WISDOM

- Agate worn as an amulet around your neck will ensure that you speak only your truth. It can also attract favors from powerful people!

- A black agate on a short chain or in a ring will ensure success in business and athletics.

- If you wear moss agate while gardening, you will have a healthy harvest.

- If you wear amazonite while gambling, you will have great luck.

- Amber will attract love into your life and increase sexual pleasure if you wear it during lovemaking.

- If a man wears an amethyst, the stone will draw a good woman to him.

- Apache tear in a pendant will protect a woman in her pregnancy.

- Frog-shaped jewelry is the ultimate traveler's amulet; pilots, stewards, sailors, and anyone who frequently travels across water should wear aquamarine in frog-shaped jewelry for enhanced safety and protection from drowning.

- Wear bloodstone in court for victory in legal matters.

- Carnelian jewelry will keep you from being struck by lightning.

- Cat's-eye worn as a ring will retain your youthful beauty and lift any depression.

- Ladies, coral earrings will attract men into your life. Pacific Islanders believe this "nature's jewel" contains the very essence of life.

- A diamond with a six-sided cut will offer you great protection; set in platinum, it will ensure victory in any conflict.

- Jade carved into the shape of a butterfly will attract love into your life.

- Lapis lazuli beads strung on gold wire will offer health, growth, and protection.

- A diamond set in onyx will overcome sexual temptation and incite the loyalty of a partner.

- Opal earrings will awaken your psychic powers.

- A red pearl ring or pendant will heighten intelligence.

- A dark peridot ring will bring you more money and raise your spirits, allaying any melancholy.

- A geode as jewelry will attract love and help a woman avoid miscarriage.

Creating Your Stone Shrine

To begin using your magical powers, you must first set the stage, the perfect environment in which to incubate your ideas. You'll do this by building a stone shrine, your touchstone for daily conjuring and contemplation. By preparing your home and sparking your inner flame, you can clear away personal blocks and invite in the friendly spirits who will aid and abet your supernatural pursuits. It is of the utmost importance to have in your home a shrine or altar, a power center, where you can keep your stones and perform rituals and spells. This is your energy source where you can renew yourself and your spirits every day. The more you use your altar, the more it will build up energy, and the more effective your spells will be.

On a low table, place a white scarf and candles from each of the colors of the spectrum: white, violet, blue, green, yellow, orange, pink, red, and black. Place them in the miraculous arching shape of a rainbow. Take amber incense and place it in a quartz crystal bowl at the center of the rainbow. Amber is good for creativity and healing and also contains crystalline grains of rock resin from Mother Nature. Keep a wand of sage or a smudging stick in a fireproof bowl or seashell on your altar and use it to clear the energy and sanctify the space every day.

Next, place symbols on the altar that reflect your personal power and spiritual aspirations. I keep fresh wildflowers in a vase beside a statue of a young goddess pouring water of wisdom, symbolizing Aquarius. I also have abalone shells, which represent my Piscean nature, aligned with a magnetite obelisk and a rock-crystal ball. Let your imagination run wild! Use religious icons and images or photos that have special meaning—whatever expresses your innermost spirit. If you have an obelisk or pyramid on your altar, you can use it for manifestation by placing your desires and wishes on paper beneath the crystal.

Keep the basic principles of feng shui in mind and put prosperity stones in your far-left money corner, and romance rocks in your far-right love corner.

The crystals you select should be a completely personal choice. Browse your favorite lapidary or New Age shop and see what you are drawn to and resonate most with. Here are some crystals you can choose for specific spell work and energy you want in your life and environment:

- **For creativity:** amazonite, aventurine, carnelian, chrysolite, chrysoprase, citrine, green tourmaline, malachite, yellow fluorite;
- **For intuition:** amethyst, azurite, celestite, lapis lazuli, moonstone, selenite, smoky quartz, sodalite, star sapphire, yellow cacite;
- **For love:** amethyst, aventurine, magnetite, rhodochrosite, rose quartz, twinned rock crystal;
- **For prosperity:** bloodstone, carnelian, citrine, dendritic agate, diamond, garnet, hawk's-eye, moss agate, peridot, ruby, tiger's-eye, topaz, yellow sapphire;
- **For self-assurance:** azurite, chalcedony, chrysocolla, green tourmaline, hematite, rutilated quartz, tiger's-eye;
- **For serenity:** amber, aventurine, blue jade, dioptase, Herkimer diamond, jasper, kunzite, moonstone, onyx, peridot, quartz, rhodonite;
- **For success:** carnelian, obsidian, quartz, selenite, sodalite, topaz;
- **For vigor:** agate, aventurine, bloodstone, calcite, chalcedony, citrine, dioptase, emerald, garnet, orange calcite, ruby, topaz;
- **For wisdom:** emerald, fluorite, Herkimer diamond, moldavite, serpentine, yellow calcite.

Chapter 3

SERENITY STONES—
CRYSTALLINE CALM
FOR YOUR HAPPY
HOME

To begin enjoying the powers of crystals in your home, you must first set the stage: the perfect environment where you experience comfort and joy. You'll do this by building a stone shrine, which will become your touchstone for daily conjuring and contemplation. By preparing your home and sparking your inner flame, you can clear away anything blocking positive energy. It is of the utmost importance to have in your home a shrine or altar, a power center, where you can keep your stones and can ponder both their power and their beauty. This is your energy source where you can renew yourself and your spirits every day.

On a low table, place a white scarf and candles from each of the colors of the spectrum: white, violet, blue, green, yellow, orange, pink, red, and black. Place them in the miraculous arching shape of a rainbow. Take your favorite incense and place it in a quartz crystal bowl at the center of the rainbow. Amber is good for creativity and healing and contains crystalline grains of rock resin from Mother Nature. Keep a wand of sage or a smudging stick in a fireproof bowl or seashell on your altar, and use it to clear the energy and sanctify the space every day.

Next, place symbols on your shrine space that reflect your personal power and spiritual aspirations. I was born on the cusp of Aquarius and Pisces, so I keep fresh wildflowers in a vase beside a statue of a young goddess pouring the water of wisdom, symbolizing Aquarius. I also have abalone shells, which represent my Piscean nature, aligned with a magnetite obelisk and a rock-crystal ball. Let your imagination run wild! Use religious icons and images or photos that have special meaning—whatever expresses your innermost spirit. If you have an obelisk or pyramid on your altar, you can use it for manifestation by placing your desires and wishes on paper beneath the crystal.

Keep the basic principles of feng shui in mind, and put prosperity stones in your far-left money corner and romance rocks in your far-right love corner.

The crystals you select should be a completely personal choice. Browse your favorite lapidary or new age shop and see what you're drawn to and resonate most with. Here are some crystals you can choose for specific spell work and energy you want in your life and environment:

- **For creativity:** amazonite, aventurine, carnelian, chrysolite, chrysoprase, citrine, green tourmaline, malachite, yellow fluorite

- **For intuition:** amethyst, azurite, celestite, lapis lazuli, moonstone, selenite, smoky quartz, sodalite, star sapphire, yellow calcite

- **For love:** amethyst, aventurine, magnetite, rhodochrosite, rose quartz, twinned rock crystal

- **For prosperity:** bloodstone, carnelian, citrine, dendritic agate, diamond, garnet, hawk's-eye, moss agate, peridot, ruby, tiger's-eye, topaz, yellow sapphire

- **For self-assurance:** azurite, chalcedony, chrysocolla, green tourmaline, hematite, rutilated quartz, tiger's-eye

- **For serenity:** amber, aventurine, blue jade, dioptase, Herkimer diamond, jasper, kunzite, moonstone, onyx, peridot, quartz, rhodonite

- **For success:** carnelian, obsidian, quartz, selenite, sodalite, topaz

- **For vigor:** agate, aventurine, bloodstone, calcite, chalcedony, citrine, dioptase, emerald, garnet, orange calcite, ruby, topaz

- **For wisdom:** emerald, fluorite, Herkimer diamond, moldavite, serpentine, yellow calcite

Rose Quartz Is Love in Mineral Form

We all get worn down now and again, and, when that happens, we often feel blue or at least in the doldrums a bit. If you have no other crystal, make sure to have rose quartz on hand. It infuses you with self-love and brightens "the vibe" anywhere it is. I view self-love as a superpower and the real foundation of all true personal power. Widely known as the stone of unconditional love, the soft pink hunk of love known as rose quartz is said to attract and inspire love in all forms. It's especially good for promoting self-love and emotional harmony. It can be a teeny tiny pebble of pink or a big ol' rock, but you should have it near you, especially when you are feeling low. I say have some around at all time, but, then again, I have crystals in every room. Keeping a piece of rose quartz out where you can see it, on your desk at work, on your bedside table, or next to the bathtub, can act as a powerful visual reminder to take a little bit of time for yourself.

Space-Clearing Crystals

To clear and purify your space and infuse it with as much of your personal energy as possible, perform a ritual sweeping with a favorite broom. I use a sweet-smelling cinnamon broom. These are actually made of pine straw coated with divine-smelling cinnamon oil and set aside to dry for three weeks. Many a grocery store sells them in the fall and holiday seasons. My favorites are the tiny Trader Joe's whisk-brooms, which are adorable. These make lovely gifts and altar adornments. I ornament mine with cleansing crystals by taking a colored silk cord and stringing quartz beads on them or gluing them to the base of the handle. These gems and crystals are superb for space-clearing and purification:

- **Amber** for positivity and happiness
- **Blue lace agate** for serenity and a peaceful home
- **Coral** for well-being and good cheer
- **Jet** absorbs bad energy from your environment
- **Onyx** is a guardian stone and protector
- **Petrified wood** for tranquility and a sense of security

- **Clear quartz** is wonderful for peace of mind and space-clearing

- **Tiger's-eye** protects from "psychic vampires," energy-draining situations or people

- **Turquoise** creates calm and relaxation

Amber

Gratitude to Mother Nature

Stones, crystals, and gems are regarded as the purest forms of the earth's generosity. Whenever you get a new crystal, receive a piece of jewelry with a stone or gem, or decorate your home or garden with rocks and pebbles, show gratitude for these gifts from nature. Simply say, "Thank you, Mother Nature, for this gift." Your gratitude will be rewarded tenfold, and you will enjoy a shower of crystals and gems in your life from our benefactress Mother Earth, who enjoys getting credit for her good works!

Amethyst

Soul-Soothing Salt Lamps

Your entryway is where things cross the threshold into your realm. Energy management starts right at the front door. One way to keep a constant vigil on this is by having a Himalayan salt lamp in your front room. Salt is one of Mother Nature's greatest protectors as it cleanses your environment of ill-omens and bad spirits. These lovely blocks of rosy-hued salt produce negative ions when warm; these ions are the very thing that makes a beach day by the ocean so cheering. A simple DIY way to have your negative ions and enjoy them too is to buy a batch of rock salt chunks at your nearby new age store or even a gourmet shop. Take a metal or wire bowl and center a small light bulb in the bottom of the bowl. Then stack the rock salt over it. You'll immediately enjoy the soft pink glow of light, and, as the rocks warm up, your mood will begin to lift. As a double benefit, the salt will constantly cleanse the energy in your home and keep it light and bright.

Soothsayer Stone: Choosing and Using a Crystal Ball

When selecting a crystal ball, your choice should not be taken lightly. This is a very personal tool that will become instilled with your energy. Crystal balls have their own authority and they can strongly influence the development of our psychic abilities. You should think of the crystal as a container that houses your energy—so make sure it feels right for you. The crystal should feel comfortable to hold—not too heavy and not too light. You should not allow anyone else to touch your crystal ball. If someone does touch it, place the ball in a bowl of sea salt overnight to cleanse it of outside energy and influence. Because quartz crystal balls have an inherent power, you have to practice working with them first. Pure quartz crystal balls can be quite expensive, but the price is worthwhile if you are serious about harnessing your intuition and using it for good. Don't expect your experiences to be like the movies. Most of the people I know who use crystal balls, including many healers and teachers, see cloudy and smoky images.

Work with a partner to sharpen your psychic skills. Sit directly across from your partner with the crystal ball between you. Close your eyes halfway and look *at* the ball and *into* the ball while harnessing your entire mind. Empty out all other thoughts and focus as hard as you can. You will sense your third eye, the traditional seat of psychic awareness, begin to open and project into the crystal ball. By practicing this way, you will train your mind. The patterns you see will become clearer and your impressions more definite. You should trust that what you are seeing is real and find a place of knowing—as I do with my stomach, which seems to be an additional center of intuition for me and I just "know in my gut" when something is off. Verbalize to your partner what you see, and then listen to your partner as she reveals her visions to you.

You should also do crystal ball meditations on your own. In a darkened room, sit and hold your crystal ball in the palms of both hands. Touch it to your heart and then gently touch it to the center of your forehead, where your third eye is located. Then hold the ball in front of your physical eyes and, sitting very still, gaze into it for at least three minutes. Envision pure white light in the ball and hold on to that image. Practice the white-light visualization for up to a half hour and then rest your mind, your eyes, and your crystal ball. If you do this every day, within a month you should start to become an adept at crystal ball gazing.

When we gaze into a crystal ball, it is possible to see into the fabric of time, both the past and the future. At first you may be able to see a flickering, wispy, suggestive image. Some of you may be able to see clearly defined visions on your first try. Most of us have to practice and hone our attunement with the energy of the ball. You must establish clearly your interpretation of what you see. Many psychics use a crystal ball in their readings, and some report seeing images of clients' auras in the ball. Projecting information about people's lives is a huge responsibility, so you need to feel sure about what you are reading. Learn to trust your body's center of intuition.

Highly polished and glasslike spheres of beryl and quartz crystal have been in use for many thousands of years. Healers, shamans, witch doctors, and medicine men have been using the bones of the earth for divination since time immemorial. The Celtic folks and Druids favored beryl as their scrying crystal of choice. Beryl still has a well-earned reputation as the stone of power. The Middle Ages and the Renaissance saw a far-flung use of crystal for seeing the future. The mythical wizard Merlin, of Arthurian legend,

SERENITY STONES—CRYSTALLINE CALM FOR YOUR HAPPY HOME

kept his crystal ball with him at all times! Pure quartz crystal balls are quite pricey, but again, are worth it if you are committed to this practice. Most people I know who use crystal balls, including many healers and teachers, see cloudy and smoky images most of the time, so do not expect your experience to immediately be like going to the movies! Each and every crystal ball is unique and has its own energy. Here are a few examples:

- **Amethyst** offers intuition on business matters and is especially good for lawyers and writers.

- **Beryl** helps you find anything you have lost—keys, jewelry, money, people!

- **Obsidian** is the karma stone and helps you see and resolve past-life issues.

- **Quartz crystal** can put you in touch with helpful spirit guides who foretell events.

- **Selenite** is particularly useful with any matters regarding hearth and home.

- **Smoky quartz** connects you with nature spirits and shows you what to avoid in your life.

Astral Azurite

The great psychic and healer Edgar Cayce used this blue beauty for achieving remarkable meditative states during which he had astoundingly accurate visions and prophetic dreams. Indeed, azurite helps achieve a high state of mental clarity and powers of concentration. If you can't find the answer to a problem in the here and now, try looking for solutions on the astral plane. Write the problem down on paper and place it under a small azurite overnight on a windowsill so it collects moonlight.

At 11:11 a.m., lie comfortably in a quiet and darkened room with the azurite stone placed over your third eye on your forehead. Clear your mind of everything for eleven minutes and meditate. Sit up and listen for the first thing that comes into your mind—it should be the answer or a message regarding the issue at hand. Write down the words you receive. The rest of the day you will be in a state of grace and higher mind during which you will hear information and answers to help guide you in many aspects of your life. If you, like me, enjoy this meditation, you may want to do it every day at 11:11 a.m. and every night at 11:11 p.m. I strongly suggest that you keep a journal of these "azurite answers." You may receive information that you won't understand until many years have passed, making the journal an invaluable resource and key to your very special life.

CRYSTAL COUNSEL

If you have ever experienced a problem in your life that no one else could help you with, a scrying mirror or crystal can offer counsel. Any time you feel the need for insight and answers, scrying can lend illumination. Are you stymied at work? Are you restless and don't know why? Do you suspect someone isn't being honest with you? Try scrying! Here are some scrying crystals to use for intuition power:

- **Amethyst** opens your own psychic abilities.

- **Azurite with malachite** can help with studying and brainstorming ideas.

- **Bloodstone** guards you against anyone trying to deceive you.

- **Celestite** gives you the very special help of angel-powered insight and advice.

- **Chrysocolla** helps you to see and resolve relationship difficulties.

- **Lapis lazuli** leads the way if you are looking for a new job.

- **Selenite** can be used under moonlight for pleasant visions of your future.

Crystal Wish Box

Keep a magic wishing box on your desk. Every so often, look at it and make a wish for your heart's desire. It's easy to make: Take a bowl or small box and fill it halfway with sand. Place these suggested wish stones in any arrangement you find pleasing.

- **Agate** for a new home

- **Amethyst** for spirituality

- **Carnelian or lapis lazuli** for a job

- **Coral** for wanting children

- **Fool's gold** for money

- **Rose quartz** for love

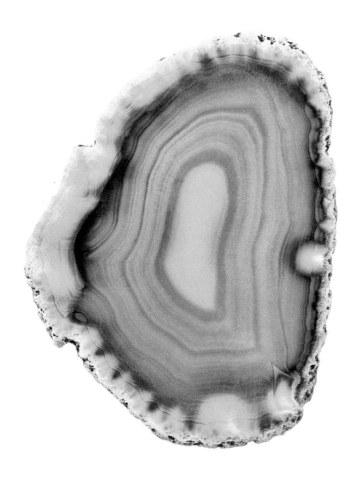

Agate

Wonderful Wands

I see many gorgeous, crystal-encrusted wands for sale in metaphysical five-and-dimes, and I am sure they are super-powered. Bear in mind, though, that it is a wonderful thing indeed to make your own wand. Start with a tree branch that has fallen to the ground on its own. Sand and polish the rough edges, as it is a wand and not a weapon. Then give it a good smudging. Hot-glue a large quartz crystal onto the wand near the handle, and hot-glue on any crystals featuring properties that will complement your magic. Citrine makes an excellent pointer tip for your wand and aligns your self-identity with your spirit. And, after all, isn't that the point? Here are stones I recommend for harnessing various powers with wands:

- **Amber** for grounding;
- **Amethyst** for balance and intuition;
- **Aventurine** for creative visualization;
- **Bloodstone** for abundance and prosperity;
- **Calcite** for warding off negativity;
- **Carnelian** for opening doors for you and helping you overcome any family problems;

- **Chalcedony** for power over dark spirits;
- **Citrine** for getting motivated and attracting money and success;
- **Fluorite** for communicating with fairies and other unseen beings;
- **Garnet** for protection from gossip;
- **Geode** for getting through periods of extreme difficulty;
- **Hematite** for strength and courage;
- **Jade** for wisdom to interpret or realize powerful dreams;
- **Jasper** for stability;
- **Lodestone** for bringing a lover back into your life;
- **Mahogany obsidian** for feeling sexy and emanating sensuality;
- **Moss agate** for powers of persuasion and healing;
- **Quartz crystal** for divining your dreams;
- **Rhodochrosite** for staying on course with your life's true purpose;
- **Rose quartz** for love;
- **Turquoise** for safety when traveling; and
- **Watermelon tourmaline** for help with planning your best possible future.

Chapter 4

POWER STONES—
FOR PROSPERITY
AND SUCCESS

Stones placed in strategic areas around your office and home can help accelerate the change you desire to bring into your life, whether that change is in your personal prosperity or being able to take care of family and loved ones. Using what I call "crystal feng shui," you can place a crystal or a geode in the appropriate position in your home to facilitate specific results. For example, amethysts will promote healing and release any negative energy that is clinging. Clusters of jade or yellow "lemon quartz" will activate vibrations of abundance and creativity.

If you want to bring more money into your home or office, place a big chunk of citrine on the left side of your desk, and the money will begin to flow! If you have a dark hallway that feels spooky or an area in your home or office in which the energy feels very static or low, place an obsidian ball there, perhaps on a pedestal, to absorb this negative energy. If you want to have your bedroom be a place of bliss and unconditional love, rose quartz will create this all-important atmosphere. Not only will these tips add to the buoyancy and joy of your home, it will also make it more striking and serene.

Obsidian

Crystal Power

- **Citrine** for stronger communication skills

- **Lace agate** for happiness with your job

- **Lapis lazuli** for mental brilliance

- **Moonstone** for self-love and self-expression

- **Red coral** for good health and physical strength

- **Rose quartz or opal** to make you appealing to others

- **Turquoise** for calmness and protection from the earth

Moonstone

Beryl Booster: Efficiency Stone

Beryl has a most unusual and important healing asset—it prevents people from doing the unnecessary. Further, it helps wearers focus, remove distractions, and therefore become calmer and more positive. Beryl also strengthens the liver, kidneys, and intestines, as well as the pulmonary and circulatory systems. It is especially effective for the throat, and pulverized beryl can be mixed into an elixir specifically for this reason. Some crystal healers use beryl along with lapis lazuli as a sedative for nervous conditions. If you get overwhelmed at work or have a huge task ahead of you, efficiency-enhancing beryl will get you through it.

Pink Beryl

How to Rock It at Work!

I am sure you will find this to be true: certain crystals can be true touchstones in your life and bring multitudinous benefits, both emotional and spiritual. Find a spot in your workspace or office where you can incorporate gemstones into your each and every day. My desk is where my crystals are placed, so I can see them often. This can be your special corner of the world where you can renew and connect with your spiritual center. Picking up and holding your touchstones can be one of the most soul-nourishing small acts of self-care you can do.

Azurite

Here are different crystals to rock at work and what they will do for you:

- **Inspiration:** amazonite, aventurine, carnelian, chrysolite, chrysoprase, citrine, green tourmaline, malachite, yellow fluorite

- **Love:** amethyst, magnetite, rhodochrosite, rose quartz, twinned rock crystals

- **Abundance:** bloodstone, carnelian, citrine, dendritic agate, diamond, garnet, hawk's-eye, moss agate, peridot, ruby, tiger's-eye, topaz, yellow sapphire

- **Intuition:** amethyst, azurite, celestite, lapis lazuli, moonstone, selenite, smoky quartz, sodalite, star sapphire, yellow calcite

- **Protection:** amber, apache tear, chalcedony, citrine, green calcite, jade, jet, smoky quartz

- **Self-belief:** azurite, chalcedony, chrysocolla, green tourmaline, hematite, rutilated quartz, tiger's-eye

- **Serenity:** amber, aventurine, blue jade, dioptase, Herkimer diamond, jasper, kunzite, moonstone, onyx, peridot, quartz, rhodonite

- **Confidence:** carnelian, obsidian, quartz, selenite, sodalite, topaz

- **Positive Energy:** agate, aventurine, bloodstone, calcite, chalcedony, citrine, dioptase, emerald, garnet, orange calcite, ruby, topaz

- **Deep Wisdom:** emerald, fluorite, Herkimer diamond, moldavite, serpentine, yellow calcite

Smoky quartz

Iron Pyrite

Fool's gold! Some of my friends say I'm a magpie, because I am so attracted to shiny objects. Let's count fool's gold, or iron pyrite, among them. I don't care if it is a hundred times less valuable than actual gold; it is very pleasing to my magpie eyes, and, every time I see it, I want to possess it. You'll be happy to know that I have restrained myself (often with the help of friends) many times. Fool's gold is usually the bright metallic yellow of its namesake but can also come in bright green and coppery colors, too. Found in North and South America, it is a crystal that has been mineralized and formed in shiny clusters.

Iron pyrite enables the skin to ward off contaminants. It is good for the respiratory system and is said to aid oxygen flow. It also has a strong connection to the iron levels in the blood and therefore benefits the circulatory system. Most people get relief from digestive aliments, too.

I treasure iron pyrite for its nearly unmatched support for personal mental workings. It boosts creativity, intelligence, logic, and the ability to communicate, while soothing fretfulness and angst. These crystal clusters radiate stability. Native Americans revered iron pyrite as a protective substance. This money-bringing and creativity-boosting stone is a must for the studios and workstations of artists, fashionistas, writers, and anyone whose artistry provides income.

Pyrite

QUICK TIP: NOT SO FOOLISH GOLD

Pyrite, or fool's gold, is the ideal heart stone for people who work with money, anyone who is an investor, banker, or money manager. Stunning and shiny, pyrite has a hardness of six, the number sacred to Venus. Pyrite brings great luck along with abundance and an atmosphere conducive to joy. Delight everyone at work by keeping a chunk of fool's gold on your desk. They will think it is a cool decoration, which is certainly is, and may never guess you have it there to ensure business is good with stable income.

Geodes

Geode jewelry can also bring you success at work. At my favorite metaphysical five-and-dimes, I have been seeing baby geodes that can easily be glued to a fabric choker band or are already in pre-made pendants. If you are feeling like you are in a slump at work or want to impress the boss, begin wearing a pretty and professional geode necklace, and things will be looking up soon! If this style is not for you, just buy a geode, set it on your desk, and look at it while picturing yourself climbing the ladder of success.

Geode half

Flourish with Fluorite: Overcome Brain Strain

Violet—or amethyst—colored fluorite is especially good for the bones, including the marrow. It jogs the third eye and, best of all, imparts good old common sense! Green fluorite is favored for its ability to ground and center excessive physical and mental energy. Clear fluorite awakens the crown chakra and allows you to let go of anything holding back spiritual development. Blue fluorite facilitates mental clarity, orderly thought, and the ability to be a master communicator. Yellow fluorite kindles the synapses and awakens memory. It will also make you smarter and boost your creativity a great deal.

Any fluorite reduces electromagnetic pollutants and cleanses the aura. Get a big chunk of fluorite at your favorite metaphysical five-and-dime, and put it right beside your computer to decrease stress. Those long hours of staring at the screen will cease to sap your energy. Look at your fluorite at least once an hour to reduce eye and brain strain, too.

Fluorite

Gifted and Talented: Success Accessories for Work

It is no accident that kings, queens, and emperors wore crowns. The ancients expected their leaders to be wise, and a bejeweled crown bestowed the brilliance and power of the gems to the crowned person, While you may not want to wear a tiara to the office or a crown to the grocery store, you can wear hair clips and barrettes with crystals and stones attached for some of the same reasons. Why not be smarter and smartly accessorized? Bejeweled barrettes worn at the temples confer wit and wisdom, a kind of brain-boosting power energy.

- **Terrific Tiger's Eye** can help you filter out mental distractions; excellent for research.

- **Tops Turquoise** is a good stone to help keep your mind and thoughts clear.

- **Fabulous Fluorite** is a true crystal of the mind and is very good for escalating mental focus.

- **Brilliant Blue Scapolite** is a beautiful blue crystal that helps with multitasking and managing a great deal of information.

- **Super Sodalite** brings clarity, insights and combines logic and intuition, a great combo!

Cords of Connection

Cord magic is one of the oldest kids of enchantments and employs a simply and powerful charm in that it can be used for any purpose in accordance with your intention. After you have set your intention, you tie a knot at each end and the cord is like a battery that holds the power of your intention as long as the knots at both end remind intact. Your magic cord is a rope that binds magic to you and is ideally made from strands of red wool or ribbon. It should be nine feet long and cut with your bolline, it is braided and tied into a loop at one end to represent feminine energy and left loose or frayed at the opposing end to signify the complementary male energy. Crystal beads woven onto the strands of the rope can compound its magical quality. I recommend that you use clear quartz crystal beads, which are energy amplifiers, but you can use special stones for various effects: rose quartz for self-love, citrine for grounding, jade for stability , blue lapis for inspiration, malachite for protection, moonstone for quiet calm, and amethyst for intuition and psychic ability.

I have an adorned cord in my bedroom on my self-care shrine that helped relieve a bout of insomnia some months ago. As I added rose quarts and amethyst beads to the red cord, I held the intention of deep rest, positive dreams, and harmony in my life. Upon knotting both ends, I have enjoyed exactly that and so can you.

Tranquility Touchstones: Crystal Cairns

I am sure you will come to find this to be true: certain crystals can be true touchstones in your life and bring multitudinous benefits, both emotional and spiritual. Find spots in your home or office where you can incorporate them each and every day. Whether it is a shrine, your nightstand, or stacked in a corner on your desk, a sort of crystal cairn. This can be your special corner of the world where you renew and connect with your spiritual center.

Picking up and holding your touchstones can be one of the most soul-nourishing small acts of self-care you can do.

The following is a table of different crystals and what their presence will bring you:

- **Inspiration**: Amazonite, aventurine, carnelian, chrysolite, chrysoprase, citrine, green tourmaline, malachite, yellow fluorite

- **Intuition**: amethyst, azurite, celestite, lapis lazuli, moonstone, selenite, smoky quartz, sodalite, star sapphire, yellow calcite

- **Love**: amethyst, magnetite, rhodochrosite, rose quartz, twinned rock crystals

- **Abundance**: bloodstone, carnelian, citrine, dendritic agate, diamond, garnet, hawk's-eye, moss agate, peridot, ruby, tigers-eye, topaz, yellow sapphire

- **Protection**: amber, apache tear, chalcedony, citrine, green calcite, jade, jet, smoky quartz

- **Self-belief**: azurite, chalcedony, chrysocolla, green tourmaline, hematite, rutilated quartz, tiger's-eye

- **Serenity**: amber, aventurine, blue jade, dioptase, Herkimer diamond, jasper, kunzite, moonstone, onyx, peridot, quartz, rhodonite

- **Confidence**: carnelian, obsidian, quartz, selenite, sodalite, topaz

- **Positive Energy**: agate, aventurine, bloodstone, calcite, chalcedony, citrine, dioptase, emerald, garnet, orange calcite, ruby, topaz

- **Deep wisdom**: emerald, fluorite, Herkimer diamond, moldavite, serpentine, yellow calcite

Chapter 5

STONE IN LOVE—
GEMS FOR
ROMANCE AND
TRUE LOVE

Since the earliest days of humankind, we have been using crystals as symbols of love. It is also true that certain stones are lucky in love and enhance and strengthen relationships. Crystals can be used for more than just tokens of affection, engagement rings, and to seal the deal on the big day of the wedding. Crystals and gems have an inherent power that can amplify existing emotions as well as create the circumstances that can cause love to bloom.

Crystal Feng Shui for Love and Happiness

Place these objects in your home to attract loving energy—new friends and relationships:

- Two crystals of rose quartz of equivalent size

- Pink, orange, or red fabric

- Two red candles

- Images of two butterflies

Jade

Jade brings with it the power of love and protection. It is also a dream stone, promoting prophetic and deeply meaningful dreams.

- **Purple jade** heals a broken heart, allowing understanding and acceptance in and pain and anger out. If you are going through a breakup, purple jade will help you with the heartache.

- **Green jade** is the counselor stone and can help troubled relationships become functional instead of dysfunctional; this shade is also a boon for the brain. Green jade helps with getting along.

- **Red jade** promotes the proper release of anger and generates sexual passion. Serve your lover a passion potion in a cup of carved red jade while wearing only red jade. Sparks will fly!

- **Blue jade** is a rock for patience, composure, and conveying a sense of control. Wear blue jade pendants for serenity.

- **Yellow jade** is for energy, simple joy, and maintaining a sense of being a part of a greater whole. A yellow jade bracelet or ring will help you feel that all is well in your world.

Green Jade

Rhodochrosite

The name simply means "rose-colored," and the color is astounding. This stone looks as if it is lit from within. It is one of the newer crystals on the scene, coming from Russia and North America. Rhodochrosite is imminently appealing, with its stripes of pink and sometimes orange.

Rhodochrosite is a love stone that will enable anyone who believes they have never truly felt or experienced real love to find it. I heard and read about some people gleaning much good from it during the aftermath of September 11. It functions as a heart-chakra opener that brings compassion and expands consciousness. One fascinating legend associated with rhodochrosite is that it can connect you to your soul mate if used in meditation. This is a crystal that helps with the healing power of forgiveness. It also helps overcome irrationality and can prevent a mental breakdown. However, I think my favorite feature of rhodochrosite is that it overcomes a poor memory. So, this rose-colored beauty banishes forgetfulness and promotes forgiveness—what a nice combination! Healers also work with this stone for respiratory diseases. It has a warm energy that is very good for the body.

This striking stone is also invaluable for overcoming fear and paranoia (mental unease). Rhodochrosite abets a more positive worldview. One of the simplest and best aspects of this crystal is that it will help you to sleep more peacefully, shoving apprehension, worry, and woe out of your mind so you can heal body and soul. Your dreams will be positive, too. This is a remarkable stone for affirming the self, allowing absolute self-acceptance and self-forgiveness. Rhodochrosite brings together the spiritual plane and the material place. The crystal is important because it permits the heart to feel hurt and pain deeply, and this processing of emotions nurtures growth.

Rhodochrosite

CRYSTAL CLOSURE

If you are having a hard time getting away from a relationship that you feel isn't good for you any longer, get closure by wearing morganite until the other person gets the message.

RELATIONSHIP RESCUE

If you and your mate are simply not getting along of late, turn to this romantic remedy rock: moonstone. Moonstone can reunite loved ones who have parted in anger. This lovely, shimmering stone also imparts luck in love. Keep moonstone around, by all means!

Amber's Emotional Healing Power

The Norse believed it to be Freya's tears that fell into the sea when she wandered the earth weeping and looking for her husband, Odin. Her tears that fell on dry land turned into golden amber. For this reason, amber is believed it to be very helpful and comforting to those who are separated and/or getting divorced, especially women, and especially those experiencing grief.

Mystical Crystal DIY: Elixir of Love

An elixir is a very simple potion made by placing a crystal or gemstone in a glass of water for at least seven hours. Then you remove the stone and drink the water, which now carries the vibrational energy of the stone, the very essence of the crystal. This is one of the easiest ways to receive crystal healing and is immediate.

The red stones always hold a lust for life. So, for the Ecstatic Elixir, we are going to push the envelope here and put as many red stones into our potion as we can! Place the following into a glass of water: carnelian, garnet, rough ruby, red coral, red jade, jasper, red sardonyx, cuprite, aventurine, and red calcite. If you don't have all of these, just mix and match. Even a single rough ruby and a tiny chunk of jasper is a lot of love in a jar.

Place the Ecstatic Elixir on the love corner of your room or altar. Light amber incense and a red candle and speak this spell: "This jade is my joy, the garnet my grace."

Leave the water on your altar for seven hour or overnight, and drink it upon awakening. Your life energy will quicken, and you should feel very upbeat and good to go.

Rocks for Romance

_____

MOONSTONE—PROPHECY AND PASSION

In olden times, it was believed that wearing a moonstone during the waning moon would offer prophetic abilities. The people of India have held moonstones as holy for thousands of years, but they had a superstition against displaying the sacred stone except on a cloth of yellow, the most spiritual color in their culture. The Indians also believed moonstone was very potent in the bedroom and not only aroused enormous passion but also gave lovers the ability to read their future together. The only problem was that they had to hold the moonstone in their mouths during the full moon to enjoy these magical properties.

OPAL—CUPID'S STONE

In the classical era, humans believed that opals were pieces of rainbows that had fallen to the ground. They also dubbed this exquisite iridescent gem Cupid's stone because they felt it looked like the love god's skin. The Arabs believed opals fell from heaven in bright flashes of lightning, thus gaining their amazing fire and color play. The Romans saw opals as symbols of purity and optimism. They believed this stone could protect people from diseases. The Roman name for opal is so beautiful and evocative—*cupid paedros,* meaning "a child as beautiful as love."

DIAMONDS—SHARDS OF THE STARS

Diamond has come to be a symbol of fidelity and is the traditional stone used in a ring for engagement, a pledge to be married and together forever. Since this gem is an aid to intuition, the ring itself will help the potential bride know if her betrothed is really "the one." Diamonds also imbue courage and can help one face anything.

EMERALDS—HEART STONES

Emerald is truly a heart stone, offering benefits on physical and emotional planes. I prefer emeralds above all other stones for engagement rings. This is your ultimate gem for happiness in a relationship. In fact, emerald has been called the stone of successful love and can engender utter felicity, total loyalty, and domestic bliss in a willing couple. The emerald is at its most powerful if worn as a pinkie—or ring—finger ornament or in a bracelet on the right wrist. But wearers, be warned! Do *not* wear emerald at all times or its super-positive force starts to reverse. A little emerald luck goes a long way.

GARNETS—THE COLOR OF LOVE

Red garnets are love stones. These sexy stones can help those with a lethargic libido tune into their passion. Green garnets are the real emotional healing stones. These crystals offer protection to the chakras. You should wear green garnets as earrings or in a necklace to get the most benefit from the inner and outer healing power.

JADE: STONE—JUST FOR LOVE

Red jade promotes the proper release of anger and also generates sexual passion. Serve your lover a passion potion in a cup of carved red jade while wearing only red jade. Sparks will fly!

JASPER—A JOLT OF LOVE ENERGY

Red jasper can bring emotions that lie beneath the surface to the forefront for healing. This stone is connected strongly to the root chakra, the source of sexual energy, and kundalini. If you would like to explore the sacred sexual practice of tantra, both partners could wear red jasper, the stone of passion. Red jasper can be a tool for rebirth and finding justice.

MALACHITE—HEART MAGIC

Malachite opens the heart and throat chakras and rebalances the solar plexus, enabling realignment of the psychic and etheric bodies. Malachite is best used as a ring on your right hand.

MOONSTONE—LUCKY IN LOVE

Moonstone opens the heart chakra and, very importantly, helps overcome any anger or hard emotions toward the self. Certain cultures have seen this as a Goddess crystal for millennia and see it as a source for nurturing, wisdom, and intuition. A moonstone is a powerfully protective and loving talisman for pregnant women. In India, moonstone is sacred and very lucky, but is even more valued in the subcontinent because it helps make you more spiritual.

Moonstone is at its very best on your behalf if worn in a ring with a silver setting.

OPAL—FIRE POWER

Opal is best worn as a pinkie ring. It is also a popular engagement ring, as it is a symbol of faithfulness and is effective in bringing stability and longevity to relationships. Fire opal is good for business by promoting positive action and prosperity. Hold your opal in your right hand and your wishes will be granted!

Rose Quartz: Self Love is the Key to Happiness

OPAL—FIRE POWER

Opal is best worn as a pinkie ring. It is also a popular engagement ring, as it is a symbol of faithfulness and is effective in bringing stability and longevity to relationships. Fire opal is good for business by promoting positive action and prosperity. Hold your opal in your right hand and your wishes will be granted!

RHODOCHROSITE—ROSE-COLORED ROMANCE

The name simply means "rose-colored," and the color is astounding. This stone seems as if it is lit from within. Rhodochrosite is a love stone that will enable anyone who believes they have never truly felt or experienced real love to find it. I heard and read about some people gleaning much good from it during the aftermath of 9/11. It functions as a heart-chakra opener that brings compassion and expands consciousness. One fascinating legend associated with rhodochrosite is that it can connect you to your soul mate if used in meditation. This is also a crystal that helps with the healing power of forgiveness.

TOURMALINE—TRUE LOVE

Purple tourmaline is a stone of devotion. Lending the highest spiritual aspirations, this crystal works by connecting the root and heart chakras. It greatly enables the ability to love unconditionally and creatively. Purple tourmaline is a heart healer.

Chapter 6

MINERAL MEDICINE— CRYSTALS FOR HEALTH AND WELLNESS

We have a vast healing and life-enhancing trove of beautiful and sacred stones from which to choose, and each stone has its own inherent, divine qualities. Each one is unique for the energy it emits and how it interacts with our subtle energy field, or aura. In the same way that no two fingerprints or snowflakes are alike, each crystal is completely individual, never to be repeated again in nature. Man-made crystals are exactly alike, thus reducing their appeal and healing qualities, at least in my mind.

Healing Stones

We have all encountered psychic vampires, whether we know it or not. Your aura will know it, because psychic vampires tear away little pieces of your *chi*, or life force, leaving holes in your aura. You can identify the places that need patching because they will become noticeably cold as you pass a crystal over them. Pick your favorite stone between amethyst, citrine, or any quartz and run it all around you at a distance of about three inches. Make note of the cold spots and lay the crystal on those places for about five minutes, until the spot feels warmer. You will have repaired the holes in your etheric body and should begin to feel a pleasant sense of renewed wholeness once again.

Here's another technique: crystal combing. It sounds odd, but you will become an aficionado immediately after you have felt the wonderfully soothing results. The beautiful pink kunzite is amazing as a mental management crystal. Take the crystal and brush it in gentle, slow, downward strokes from the top of your head, the crown chakra, to the bottom of your feet. The next time you feel overwhelmed by anxiety, try this and you will feel more relaxed and in control afterward.

Kunzite is also a heart mender which touches upon the heart chakra to bring inner peace, clear away old romantic wounds, and get rid of emotional baggage. You can place a chunk of kunzite upon your chest and meditate with it to feel the healing energy flow in.

Cranium-Calming Crystals

Lapis lazuli has been used to treat headaches for millennia. My dear friend Abby suffers from migraines and cluster headaches. I gave her some earrings with lovely blue lapis settings to help her with this chronic condition, and she has reported great success. These headaches can have many causes and triggers; my beloved amber essence oil was one until we figured that out! The main causes are stress, anxiety, and various food triggers. Oddly enough, amber in crystal form alleviated Abby's heinous headaches, seemingly absorbing the negative energy. Amethyst and turquoise are also good for this. Several stones are good for stomach illnesses, including citrine and moonstone which create calm that, in this case, stops the stomach unrest from signaling the brain to have a headache.

Laying on of Stones

This healing practice is distilled from the study of chakras. Here are just a few examples of how to apply stones directly to your body or that of anyone else who needs healing. After you have gotten the knack of it, you can use the information in this book to try your own healing applications of stones and gems.

The first step for anyone undertaking crystal healing is to lie down, relax, and get very comfortable. Empty everything else from your mind.

Lapis lazuli and its fellow blue aquamarine can be laid upon the throat chakras to release any blockage therein. This greatly aids in self-expression and is wonderful for professional speakers as well as performers such as actors and singers. Turquoise laid on the face—cheeks, forehead, and chin—is a calming agent, significantly reducing tension. Azurite on the brow opens the third eye and deepens wisdom; this can balance the energy of the head and allow more light into the third eye.

Malachite, a heart stone, placed near the heart and along the center of the abdomen will create a sense of harmony and facilitate letting go of pain, suffering, and old childhood wounds.

Malachite

Darning Your Aura: Crystal Combing

We have all encountered psychic vampires, whether we know it or not. The problem is, your aura will know it because psychic vampires tear away little pieces of your *chi*, or life force, leaving holes in your aura. You can identify the places that need patching because they will become noticeably cold as you pass a crystal over them. Pick your favorite stone from amethyst, citrine, or any quartz and run it all around you at a distance of about three inches. Make note of the cold spots and lay the crystal on those places for about five minutes, until the spot feels warmer. You will have repaired the holes in your etheric body and should being to feel a pleasant sense of renewed wholeness once again.

Here's another technique: crystal combing. It sounds odd, but you will become an aficionado immediately after you have felt the wonderfully soothing results. The beautiful pink kunzite is amazing as a mental management crystal. Take the crystal and brush it in gentle, slow, downward strokes from the top of your head, the crown chakra, to the bottom of your feet. The next time you feel overwhelmed by anxiety, try this and you will feel more relaxed and in control afterward.

CHAKRA CRYSTALS

The concept of chakras originated many thousands of years ago in Asia. The ancient philosophers and metaphysicians identified seven main energy centers around the body and saw each chakra emanating energy in the form of a rainbow color that affected the mental, physical, and spiritual balance in a human being. Chakra theory is the basis of many Eastern healing practices. One of the simplest ways to achieve well-being is to place crystals on the parts of the body where certain chakras are centered. Many people I know credit their clarity and well-being to chakra therapy. One sure way to relieve stress and fortify the emotional body is this laying on of crystals.

Chakra	Color	Energies	Corresponding Crystals
First, root (base of spine)	Red	Security, Survival	Garnet, Smoky Quartz
Second, sacral	Orange	Pleasure	Amber, Carnelian
Third, solar plexus	Yellow	Drive, Personal Power	Amber, Citrine, Topaz
Fourth, heart	Green	Abundance, Love, Serenity	Peridot, Rose Quartz
Fifth, throat	Blue	Creativity, Originality	Blue Quartz, Tiger's-Eye
Sixth, third eye	Indigo	Intuitiveness, Perception	Fluorite, Lapis Lazuli
Seventh, crown	Violet	Holy Bliss, All Is One	Amethyst, Diamond

Rainbow Renewal

The rainbow is a simple and effective method for total-body wellness. Choose from this list of stones, making sure you have one of each color of the rainbow—violet, indigo, blue, green, yellow, orange, and red—plus one white stone and one black stone for completion. Then, simply lay the stones on their corresponding chakra centers; the rainbow should travel up your body. Red for your root chakra, orange for your sacral chakra, yellow for your solar plexus chakra, green for your heart chakra, blue for your throat chakra, indigo for your third eye chakra, and violet for your crown chakra. I've included a list of crystal and body affinities in case there is any specific area you want to focus on:

- **Amber** for the thyroid

- **Benitoite** for the pituitary

- **Beryl** for the eyes

- **Bloodstone** for the kidneys

- **Blue tourmaline** for the thymus

- **Brown jasper** for the shins and for the skin

- **Calcite** for the skeletal system

- **Carnelian** for the liver

- **Celestite** for the intestines

- **Chalcedony** for the spleen

- **Chrysocolla** for the pancreas

- **Chrysolite** for the appendix

- **Chrysoprase** for the prostate

- **Danburite** for the muscles

- **Dendrite agate** for the nervous system

- **Dioptase** for the lungs

- **Fire agate** for the stomach

- **Fluorite** for the teeth

- **Garnet** for the spine

- **Hematite** for the blood and circulatory system

- **Jadeite** for the knees

- **Lapis lazuli** for the throat

- **Magnetite** for the joints

- **Moldavite** for the hands

- **Moonstone** for the womb area

- **Orange calcite** for the bladder

- **Purple fluorite** for the bone marrow

- **Rose quartz** for the heart

- **Smoky quartz** for the feet

Blue tourmaline

MYSTICAL CRYSTAL DIY: SWEEPING CHANGE

To purify your home, you need this special broom. A home purification is handy for clearing away bad energy after a squabble with your loved one, a bout of the blues, or just about any upset you need to get out of your personal space. I would go so far as to suggest that you sweep the negative energy outside every morning in your life. Bear in mind, this is not white glove-type cleaning; it is a symbolic act that is quite effective in maintaining your home as a personal sanctuary.

You can make your own purification broom from straw bound together and attached to a fallen tree branch, or you can add mojo to a store-bought broom. Wrap copper wire around your broom or use it to bind the straw to the stick, as Venus-ruled copper lends an aura of beauty and keeps negativity at bay. Attach crystals to the handle with glue to boost your broom. Recommend crystals for space clearing and purification are:

- **Amber** for cheeriness;
- **Blue lace agate** for tranquility;
- **Coral** for well-being;

- **Jet** for absorption of bad energy;
- **Onyx** for protection;
- **Petrified wood** for security;
- **Tiger's-eye** for protecting your psyche from energy draining powers; and
- **Turquoise** for relaxation and calmness.

The Secret to Thomas Edison's Genius: Dream Crystals

Thomas Edison carried quartz crystals with him at all times and called the stones his dream crystals. He believed they inspired his ideas and inventions. Literary legends George Sand and William Butler Yeats also relied on crystals to help spark their considerable creativity.

Data has also been gathered to show the effectiveness of quartz in certain healing techniques, such as chakra therapy, acupressure, and light-ray therapy. However, the simplest way to promote healing with crystals is to wear a stone.

Quartz

Quartz can take the form of great hexagonal stones or of crystals so small that only a microscope can see them. Quartz can appear in clusters or singly. It can also appear in every hue of the rainbow. The gorgeous and varied hues of quartz come from electrostatic energy, which now can be altered through technology. I, however, prefer the simple beauty provided by Mother Nature herself.

Quartz is the largest of the crystal families, and we can be grateful for that since it is such a powerful healer. Moreover, it is an energy regulator for the human body, affecting the vibrations of the *aura*, or energy field that surrounds all living beings.

Pain Relief Prisms

When you feel pain somewhere in your body, it is a small voice that needs to be listened to. It could be old energy that needs to be released, a blockage, or an imbalance. Many years ago, I was hit by a drunk driver who plowed through a red light and totaled my car, and very nearly me. As I hit the brake, my foot and ankle were shattered, rather like a porcelain teacup thrown with great force. The doctors wanted to amputate my leg, but I managed to talk them out of it. I had to learn to walk again, but I can walk, dance, and even run after lots of physical therapy and healing. But, nowadays, whenever I hit the brake too hard, I feel pain because my body remembers. The tissue and bones hold the memory imprint of that awful day and the terrible trauma.

Crystals have very mild and serene ways of tranquilizing negative energy and releasing the pain. In my case, I ever so gently rub a crystal across my ankle. (Carnelian works well because it is said to be good for healing bones, but quartz can also serve the purpose.) The stone feels cool and calming as the pain dissipates. I can also visualize the pain going into the crystal and the crystal forming a prism that contains the pain. At first, this was very frightening for me, but I found that rose quartz helped me deal with my fear. I placed the rose quartz over the heart area, the solar plexus, and, as the crystal touched upon the heart chakra, I felt the fear dissolving while the pain gradually lessened. Turquoise and carnelian are also good for this.

I once had a copper bracelet set with onyx, coral, and turquoise from a Cherokee reservation that was so effective at treating wrist pain that it finally disintegrated from overuse. Copper is unmatched for dealing with edema, the swelling and inflammation that can be caused by arthritis, repetitive stress injuries, sports-related soreness, and many other issues.

Malachite has a lot of the mineral copper in it, so a pendant, ring, or bracelet with malachite can be a great agent for pain reduction. Iron-rich magnetite is another pain absorber.

Earth Stones for Centering: Grounding and Healing Gems and Crystals

Jasper Stone: This stone has been valued for its healing and grounding energies since ancient times. These healing crystals carry a very strong earthly energy, helping to deepen your personal connection with the earth when you wear or meditate with these grounding crystals. I recommend either brown or red jasper, both of which are healing stones that also give you great strength, heighten energy, and have a lovely reinvigorating effect on your body.

Hematite: This stone is a deeply grounding crystal for the body. It has a high density and even it is a relatively small pebble; it will feel heavier in your hand than you might expect. Hematite contains tremendous grounding energy that literally feels like you are one with the Earth. Touch it to your skin, and you will feel a magnetic energy. It is this effect that will make you feel more balanced, calm, and centered. Hematite stones also soak up any negative energy within your body or energy field. After you have used it, you should place the stone in a bowl of pure salt to cleanse it.

Smoky Quartz Stone: Smoky quartz is another beautifully grounding and stabilizing crystal that brings powerful energies for centering the body. This particular quartz has the effect of making you feel deeply rooted to the earth. It is very centering in an uplifting way, having a much more subtle energy than Hematite. Smoky quartz works to counteract any negative vibrations, replacing them with the positive.

K2 Stone: This crystal has recently become more popular as it brings new discovery and revelation for many. K2 is a combination of grounding granite and celestial *Azurite*, which balances our earthbound life experiences with our higher consciousness and connection to the universe and the heavens. It is an extremely powerful way to connect to your intuition and find the balance between your intuition and your daily life. If you are wrestling with a real issue in your life or need to make a difficult choice when the options are unclear to you, call upon K2 and use it in meditation. Soon, the answers will come.

Shungite Stone: Here is the most powerful stone for balancing. Shungite will inspire you to deal with your emotions, toxic mental thoughts, and anything that no longer serves you. While it can be unpleasant to look at these personal issues, it is, in actuality, a healthy thing to do. What you gain from this exercise is the grace and strength to cut the energetic cords that hold you back from your personal power.

Shungite stone

Chapter 7

CRYSTAL CHARMS—
HOW TO CHOOSE
AND MAKE
CHANGE-YOUR-
LIFE JEWELRY

Gems are powerful tools that can pave the way to a better life. There is a long history of the use of gems, stones, and crystals as amulets, symbols, charms, and jewelry in magic. These myriad stones can really enrich your life in so many ways. In this chapter, you will learn how to make your own magical gem and crystal jewelry and how to charge the stones you already own with supernatural power. Do you want to get a new job? Jade jewelry magic will do the trick! Need to get over a heartbreak? A chrysocolla heart-healing pendant will soothe your soul. This chapter will show you how you can accessorize to not only enhance your appearance but enhance your life!

Necklaces, Pendants, and Chokers

Perhaps you want to be a better communicator or vocalist or simply want to express yourself more freely. A blocked throat chakra can result in your feelings and ideas being blocked. So, in this case, you will want to focus on opening it up. A necklace or choker can serve this purpose. A strand of pearls not only looks timelessly elegant but also boosts your self-esteem and sociability. The best metals for this use are silver, copper, and gold. You will want to avoid aluminum entirely because it is considered to be a health risk.

Speaking Stones

If you are a singer or speaker or simply wish to improve how you express yourself, wear these stones in chokers or necklaces to realize a noticeable change for the better: amber, amethyst, aquamarine, azurite, blue obsidian, blue topaz, blue tourmaline, kunzite, lepidolite, and turquoise.

Lepidolite

DIY Crystal Charm

This "floating" crystal choker seems magical because the gems appear to hover around your lovely neck all by themselves. And maybe sometimes they do! The secret, aside from the magical gems, is the invisible thread, easily obtained at any craft store. The purpose of the Choker of Charm is to make you simply irresistible to whomever you wish to attract. Wake your boyfriend up with this enchanted choker, or hit the town with your friends and notice how a crowd develops around YOU!

You'll need these ingredients: twenty-one crystal beads, twenty-two inches of invisible thread, a lobster-claw clasp, and glue.

First, tie one end of the invisible thread to the loop in the lobster-claw clasp, also readily available at any craft store and most jewelry stores. Knot the thread twice, add a drop of glue, and allow the thread to dry. Clip off the extra thread after the glue has dried. Then, string three beads onto the thread about three-quarters of an inch from the clasp and tie a knot in the thread beside the beads. Repeat until you have used all the beads. There will be seven groups of three, and each group of crystals should be evenly separated. At the last bead, tie the end of the thread to the clasp ring.

Here are a few irresistible crystals to consider using in your Choker of Charm:

- **Amazonite** makes you hopeful

- **Amber** boosts your spirits—you will feel good!

- **Aventurine** creates good opportunities

- **Banded agate** attracts a lover of strength and courage

- **Brown jasper** makes you confident and emotionally secure

- **Opal** enhances beauty and makes you more psychic

- **Pearl** augments femininity

Amazonite

Earring Elegance

You can wear one gold earring and one silver earring to rid yourself of the discomfort of a headache. Earrings were once worn to guard ears from potential disease and from hearing bad news. They were also believed to strengthen weak eyes, especially if set with emeralds. Earrings help to balance both hemispheres of the brain and can stabilize the throat chakra. The earlobes are sensory centers of the body and usually benefit from the stimulation of a gem or crystal. Jade and tiger's-eye are great for reviving and refreshing. You will generally feel quite good with these two earring choices. Sapphires will bring you greater wisdom. However, lapis lazuli and opal can be overstimulating as earrings, so watch carefully and see how your body reacts to them. Some people feel light-headed with these two stones placed so high on the body. Malachite can be too spiritually stimulating when set in earrings; don't wear them unless you want to be in a soulful or dreamy reverie. Go for garnet, as garnet earrings will enhance your popularity. Here is a tip that might soon cause a stampede to the jewelry shop: rose quartz is wonderful for the skin and can even slow aging!

Jewelry That Protects You and Your Loved Ones: Amulets

The term "amulet" comes from the Latin word meaning "defense." Indeed, amulets are a way to protect yourself that dates back from the earliest human beliefs. Pliny himself subscribed to the use of amulets and wrote about three common kinds used by the Romans of the classical age. A typical amulet of that era was a bit of parchment inscribed with protective words, rolled up in a metal cylinder, and worn around the neck. Evil eyes might be the most global of all amulets, the belief being that they could ward off a hex by simply reflecting it back to its origins. Phallic symbols have always been popular, too, coming in the shapes of horns, hands, and the phallus, of course. Some amulets were devoted to a specific god or goddess, and the wearer of such a piece would be protected by that divine entity.

The peoples of the Mesopotamian plain wore amulets. The Assyrians and Babylonians favored cylindrical seals encrusted with precious stones. They also loved animal talismans for the qualities associated with different animals: lions for courage, bulls for virility, and so on. The ancient Egyptians absolutely depended on their amulets for use in burial displays, and we can see many preserved in the cases of today's museums. To make their amulets, the Egyptians employed a material called faience, a glazed composition of ground quartz that was typically blue green in color. Wealthier denizens of the Nile, royalty, and the priestly class wore precious and semiprecious gems and crystals as amulets. Lapis lazuli was perhaps the most revered of these and was worn in many shapes, the eye of Horus being the most significant religious icon, followed by the scarab symbolizing rebirth; the frog, symbolizing fertility; and the ankh, representing eternal life.

Organized religions appropriated the idea of amulets from pagan peoples, and it was very popular in medieval times to wear a tiny verse from the Torah, the Bible, or the Koran. Today, many a Catholic wears a medal honoring a given saint, such as Saint Christopher, the patron saint for travelers. Wiccans and modern pagans are great proponents of protective amulets, causing a resurgence in Celtic symbols and imagery.

Amulets are very easy to create and make nice gifts, as long as you believe your friends will truly benefit from them and are aware of the special qualities and powers they hold. To make one, select a crystal that is endowed with the desired energy. Hold it in the palm of your hand until it is warm from your touch. Then, visualize the specific power the stone is offering. If you're giving your amulet to yourself, wear it as a pendant or tuck it into your pocket or purse for a "guardian to go." Here is a list of stones from which to choose for the specific kind of safeguard you are in need of:

- **Amethyst** helps with sobriety by preventing inebriation.

- **Aquamarine** is good for attracting wisdom and overcoming a fear of water and drowning. It is also a guard against malevolent spirits.

- **Bloodstone** brings luck and is good to wear during travels.

- **Carnelian** is to the devil as garlic is to a vampire—keeps him away!

- **Chrysolite** drives away evil spirits and promotes peaceful sleep, especially if set in gold.

- **Diamond** in a necklace brings good fortune and lends force and valor. This dazzling stone should always touch the skin and works best when it is received as a gift.

- **Emerald** can cancel out the power of any magician!

- **Jade** offers protection, especially for children, and guards their health. It also creates prosperity.

- **Jasper** is reputed to be a defense against the venom of poisonous insects and snakes.

- **Jet** set in silver will help expel negativity.

- **Moonstone** is another boon to travelers and brings fortune and fame.

- **Turquoise** is believed to be great for a horse's gait if affixed to the animal's bridle.

TALISMANS

A talisman is decorative object, or *objet*, that also provides protection and has magical properties. A talisman can be any article or symbol that you believe has mystical qualities. As we know, many gems and crystals have special innate powers. With a talisman, the special powers can be naturally present or instilled during a ritual. People often confuse amulets with talismans, but they differ in this significant way: Amulets *positively protect* the wearer from harm, evil, and negativity. Talismans *actively transform* the wearer to have certain powers. For example, the supernatural sword Excalibur, imbued with supremacy by the Lady of the Lake, gave King Arthur magical powers.

Grimoires (spell books) offer instruction on making talismans. The reasons for using talismans are many—for love, for wealth, for luck with gambling, for the gift of a silver tongue, for a good memory, for the prevention of death. Whatever you can think of, there is probably a talisman for that exact purpose!

Sacred Stone Shapes

- **Ankh**-shaped stones represent the key to life. Use this ancient Egyptian symbol to develop creativity, wisdom, and fertility.

- **Clusters** are among the most common natural crystal forms and bring balance and harmony into your life.

- **Diamond**-shaped stones bring the energy of wealth and abundance and are said to attract riches.

- **Egg**-shaped stones denote creativity and give new ideas to anyone wearing them.

- **Heart**-shaped stones bring love energy. They promote self-love and romance.

- **Holes** that form naturally in stones are very auspicious and magical. If you look through the holes by the light of the moon, you should see visions and spirits.

- **Human body**-shaped stones bring good energy to the body parts being depicted and strengthen those areas.

- **Obelisks** are four-sided, pyramid-topped shapes and are wonderful energy activators, or manifestors. Write your wish down on paper and place it beneath an obelisk to bring that hope into reality.

- **Octahedrons**, eight-sided stones, bring order to chaos and are great for analysis and organization. They are also terrific for healing. Carry an octahedron crystal in your pocket if you are unwell, so you can feel better soon.

- **Pyramid**-shaped stones carry energy upward, toward their pointed tips. I have a beautiful little malachite pyramid that I keep on my computer simply because I love to look at it. When the need arises, however, I can place a dollar bill underneath it and visualize positive money energy flowing up out of the stone.

- **Rectangular** rocks and crystals represent the energy of God. In addition to symbolizing male energy and the phallus, this shape is symbolic of energy itself and electrical current. It also denotes protection. Rectangular stones are great for love and sex spells.

- **Round** stones represent the universe and the Goddess. They are symbols of spirituality, connection to the universe, femininity, and, of course, pregnancy. Round crystals can be used in all love spells to cause attraction.

- **Square** stones represent the earth and are harbingers of plenty and prosperity.

- **Triangular** stones are guardian stones and protect the wearers.

Pearls for Patience

In this fast-paced world, we are so accustomed to instant gratification (thanks, high-speed internet and same-day deliveries). We are multitasking ourselves to death. Slow down and enjoy your life. It is worth it, I assure you. Here is a quick way to simply relax and enjoy the little things in life: wear a pearl. Pearl earrings and necklaces are the best, as they calm and clear the mind.

Pearl necklace

Chains of Being

Chains represent links between people, the ties that bind you to others. Other mystical associations for chains are happiness and justice, prayer, reason and the soul, and communication and command. Plato referred to a *chain of being*, a golden chain linking the earth to the heavens above, a bond between humans and immortals. Socrates tied our human happiness to the concept of justice with a chain of steel and diamonds. Pseudo-Dionysius the Areopagite compared the practice of prayer to an infinitely luminous chain going from earth to heaven. An astral cord, akin to a golden chain, binds the spirit to the psyche and binds reason to the soul. Because of this, gold chains are extremely powerful symbols.

Gold chain

Kiss My Ring

Opal ring

Rings represent eternity, unity, reincarnation, safety, union, power, and energy. They symbolize the eternity of the circle shape and its summation—the universe. Wearing rings was believed to help ward off any kind of malevolence through their continuity. Nothing could get past this strong, flawless circle. A ring binds you with the energy of the stone. In dream psychology, a ring represents the desire for reconciliation of the different parts of your being and personality; it shows you want to be an integrated whole, which is the first step in making it happen. If you want to deepen a friendship, exchange amber rings with your friend to bind you together forever. Why do you think Native Americans wear turquoise rings? They know it is a guardian stone; its power is doubled when it is in a ring.

When wearing a ring, be sure the bottom side of the stone is open to allow greater connection between the stone and your skin. On your left hand, wear ring gems that awaken and release emotions, and, on your right hand, wear stones that will enhance your career and your personal goals in life. I know that thumb rings have become a big trend, but you should know that wearing them could block the energy of the thumbs or, even worse, bring out egotism and selfishness.

Your index fingers are indicators of achievement, and wearing the proper gem on that finger can really aid you in striving for your dreams. For wisdom, wear lapis lazuli. For greater love of yourself and others, try pearl, moonstone, or garnet. For success, wear carnelian. For a quiet mind and greater calm, wear sodalite, chrysocolla, or turquoise.

Your middle fingers are about ideas and insights, as well as intuition; the left hand represents the receiving of ideas, and the right hand represents action and achievement in your life. Wear stones on the middle finger only when you want to get a lot of psychic input from the world around you. For greater sensitivity and creativity, wear amethyst. To awaken your inner and outer beauty, wear ruby. To access your higher good and know your life's purpose, wear sapphire or quartz crystal.

The ring finger is about creativity, and, of course, the ring finger on the left hand is your love center and a direct connection to your heart. For deep and loyal ties of love, wear diamond. To express your love, wear moonstone. To inspire creativity, wear emerald. To meet creativity goals, wear tiger's-eye or cat's-eye. For practicality in your work and art, wear turquoise. For service to your community and the world, wear opal. For both inner and outward serenity, wear ruby.

Pinkie fingers represent change. The right gem on your little finger can help you find and pursue new opportunities and change the direction of your whole life. This is a lot of power in one little ring! For better organizational habits, wear pearl. For unwinding and simplifying, wear turquoise. To bring new energy and new prospects, wear aventurine.

Turquoise ring

MYSTICAL CRYSTAL DIY: MESSAGE IN A BOTTLE

In use since Elizabethan times, magic bottles, or spell bottles, can function as guardians. Called witch bottles in the 1600s in England, they were originally used to hold objects for magical uses. They have largely fallen out of use, but you can customize magic bottles for yourself with crystal stoppers for a variety of reasons. You can put one in your garden for healthy plants, on the mantel to protect your home, next to your bed for love and happiness, and in the kitchen for good health. These magic bottles are mostly used for protection, but you can also place into them symbols of your dreams and desires, such as a flower for peace, rosemary for remembrance, and cinnamon for the spice of life.

Magic bottles are very easy to make, as you can easily glue the crystals of your choice onto the lid or cork top or place them inside. Here are a few to try:

For **luck** with money, place three pennies and some pyrite or jade into a bottle and put it on your desk and home or your workplace. Shake the magic jar whenever you think about your finances, and your fortune will improve in three days.

For **love**, place a rosebud or rose petal, rose essential oil, and rose quartz into a bottle and keep it at your bedside. Each night, burn a pink candle anointed with the oil from your love-magic bottle. On the seventh day, your prospects for romance will brighten!

For a **peaceful** and **secure** home, take a teaspoon of soil from outside your house (or the closest park) and place it into a bottle with some smoky topaz or brown jasper. Place the bottle into the pot of a plant near the entrance of your home. Every time you water the plant, think about the sanctity of your home. As your plant grows, so will the tranquility of your residence.

Labradorescence: Activate Your Third Eye

Labradorite is a stunning stone with a lovely iridescence. As a magpie who is attracted to shiny objects, it grabs my attention every time. It can look as dull as dirt until you give it a closer examination; then you can see the glow under the surface. When cut and polished, it is fascinating and gorgeous, with an impressive light show including yellows, oranges, blues, and violets. In fact, the special play of light and color across the surface is called labradorescence. The effect is caused by lamellar intergrowths, which were produced inside the crystal while the crystal formed during a shift of temperature from extremely high to very low. Named for the place it was first found, Labrador, this loveliest of shiny objects can also be found in India, Finland, Russia, Newfoundland, and Madagascar.

As you might guess, this bluish feldspar is a soul stone with a very powerful light energy. It abets astral travel, the higher mind, and intelligence and is a favorite of mystics. It brings up nothing but the positive for the brain and consciousness and excises the lower energies of anxiety, stress, and negative thoughts. It is an aura cleanser and balancer. Labradorite, which used to be called spectrolite, also protects against aura leakage. This is a crystal to hold and keep with your during meditation for psychic flashes, much like the flashes of light from within the stone.

I had no idea that it is also a stone that awakens psychic powers and activates your third eye until I learned this from

CRYSTAL CHARMS—HOW TO CHOOSE AND MAKE CHANGE-YOUR-LIFE JEWELRY

the great teacher Scott Cunningham. Even a small piece of this special crystal will work. Take the crystal and hold it to the center of your forehead with both hands. Speak aloud:

Artemis, Astarte, Athena, Circe—fill me with your power,
On this day, I ask you lend me your seer's vision.
I stand at the threshold in this holy hour.
And so it is. Great goddesses; I am grateful.

Seven Sacred Stones Bracelet

Take any silver chain-link bracelet and add "charm" to it! Bracelets act as protection jewelry, and, well, they look simply divine on our delicate wrists, do they not? Of late, the trend has been to layer bracelets, but, with gem magic, there's a danger that jeweled pieces worn together could cancel each other out because they have conflicting energies. So, I'm going to recommend that you wear this bracelet alone, without other magical wrist wear.

To make this piece, you'll need seven stones on small pendent settings, a silver chain-link bracelet, seven jump rings, and pliers. Plain silver chain-link bracelets are easy to obtain at any jewelry department or store, from Target to Tiffany. Jump rings are open rings onto which you can slide a pendant and then close up with small chain-nose pliers. They are readily available at any craft or jewelry store.

Before you choose your seven stones, decide what energy enhancement you desire. If you want lots of energy and zest, choose red jasper or pink clamshell. If you want to be uplifted, try jade. To become wiser, pick sapphire. To stay safe while traveling, pick dendritic agate. To remain calm and overcome stress, choose blue lace agate. For more mental clarity, choose malachite. For a self-esteem boost, try rhodonite.

Once you have pursued all the gem and crystal descriptions in this book, you can and should experiment with all manner of combinations. However, I highly recommend the Seven Sacred Stones Bracelet with the following very beneficial stones and energies:

- **Citrine** for a better ability to communicate

- **Lace agate** for happiness with your job

- **Lapis lazuli** for mental brilliance

- **Moonstone** for self-love and self-expression

- **Red coral** for good health and physical strength

- **Rose quartz or opal** to make you appealing to others

- **Turquoise** for calmness and protection from the earth

Friends of mine have reported wonderful results with this banishing and boosting bracelet. Where else can you find jewelry that will make you feel good about yourself, protect you from harm, and help you to look even prettier? You have to make it! You can find these pendant-set stones in any jewelry or new age store. The metaphysical stores have the best selection, however.

Citrine

Conclusion

CRYSTAL POWER

With crystal power, you can improve your life in ways large and small. You've discovered the stones that are special to you, and how to fully utilize these birthstones and karmic crystals. You have received advice for crystal healing and stress-dispersing. You've heard how gems and statues positioned in strategic places around your home or workspace can help accelerate the positive vibrations you are activating in your life. Using what I have called crystal feng shui, you can place a crystal, geode, or appealingly shaped rock in the appropriate position in your home or workspace to facilitate change. Having different gemstones or crystals within easy reach can bring you clarity, patience, and inspiration when you need it the most.

Yes, through the power and positive energy of crystals, anything is possible. With the information in this book, I hope you can gather together the stones and crystals that sing the loudest to you and integrate them into your life. May this glittering and magical realm make you welcome, and may you and your loved ones enjoy the many blessings of these sacred stones!

Nephrite

About the Author

Cerridwen Greenleaf has worked with many of the leading lights of the spirituality world including Starhawk, Z Budapest, John Michael Greer, Christopher Penczak, Raymond Buckland, Luisah Teish, and many more. She gives herbal workshops throughout North America. Greenleaf's graduate work in medieval studies has given her deep knowledge she utilizes in her work, making her unique in the field. She lives, gardens, and works in San Francisco.

Make sure to check out her inspiring blogs below:

- www.witchesandpagans.com/pagan-culture-blogs/ middle-earth-magic.html

- www.yourmagicalhome.blogspot.com/

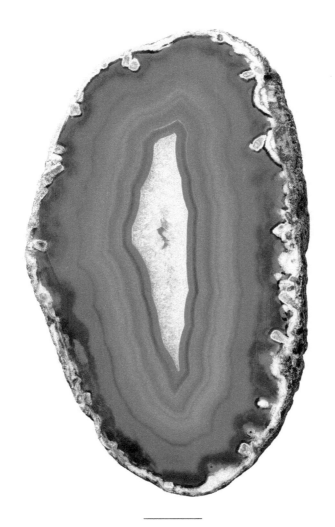

Violet Agate

BOOKS FOR A MAGICAL LIFE FROM CERRIDWEN GREENLEAF

ISBN 978-1-63353-533-6
PRICE $18.95
TRIM 6x9

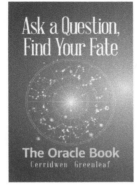

ISBN 978-1-63353-565-7
PRICE $16.95
TRIM 5.5x8.25

ISBN 978-1-63353-535-0
PRICE $18.95
TRIM 6x9

ISBN 978-1-63353-562-6
PRICE $18.95
TRIM 6x9

ISBN 978-1-63353-792-7
PRICE $18.99
TRIM 5.5x8.5

ISBN 978-1-63353-872-6
PRICE $18.99
TRIM 5.5x8.5

www.ingramcontent.com/pod-product-compliance
Lightning Source LLC
Jackson TN
JSHW061343131224
75386JS00052B/1800